IN LOVE

IN LOVE

A Memoir of
Love and Loss

Amy Bloom

RANDOM HOUSE
NEW YORK

Copyright © 2022 by Amy Bloom

Published in the United States by Random House, an imprint and division
of Penguin Random House LLC, New York.

RANDOM HOUSE and the HOUSE colophon are registered trademarks
of Penguin Random House LLC.

Grateful acknowledgment is made to Houghton Mifflin Harcourt Publishing
Company for permission to reprint "Allegro ma Non Troppo" from *Map:
Collected and Lost Poems* by Wisława Szymborska, translated from the Polish
by Stanisław Barańczak and Clare Cavanagh. English translation copyright
© 2015 by Houghton Mifflin Harcourt Publishing Company. Reprinted by
permission of Houghton Mifflin Harcourt Publishing Company.

Library of Congress Cataloging-in-Publication Data
Names: Bloom, Amy, author.
Title: In Love / Amy Bloom.
Description: First edition. | New York: Random House, 2022.
Identifiers: LCCN 2021008876 (print) | LCCN 2021008877 (ebook) | ISBN
9780593243947 (hardcover) | ISBN 9780593243961 (ebook)
Subjects: LCSH: Ameche, Brian A.—Mental health. | Alzheimer's disease—
Patients—Biography. | Alzheimer's disease—Patients—Family relationships.
Classification: LCC RC523.3. B66 2022 (print) | LCC RC523.3 (ebook) |
DDC 616.8/3110092 [B]—dc23
LC record available at https://lccn.loc.gov/2021008876
LC ebook record available at https://lccn.loc.gov/2021008877

Printed in the United States of America on acid-free paper

randomhousebooks.com

2 4 6 8 9 7 5 3 1

First Edition

Book design by Susan Turner

For Brian

"Please write about this," my husband said.

PART I

Sunday, January 26, 2020, Zurich, Switzerland

This trip to Zurich is a new, not quite normal version of something Brian and I love: traveling. Road trip, train ride, ferry ride, airplane anywhere. We like all travel and most shopping, and this trip to Zurich has all the accoutrements of our other trips and is also nothing like anything we've ever done. As we usually do, we take a car service to the airport so we can be fancy and also avoid the park-and-schlep, and even before Brian had Alzheimer's, our combined lack of direction adds twenty minutes to all transportation transitions. We have a restaurant meal before our 6 P.M. departure. I buy a stick of lipstick and a small tube of hand cream; Brian buys some candy. We share gum. We share a bottle of water.

On the plane, we enjoy the settling in, the attention of the flight attendants, who already like us because Brian is mindful about his size and doesn't swing his arm into someone else's drink and he expresses appreciation to every single Swissair representative. We seem like people who will not be screaming for more booze or more peanuts at midnight. No one loves business class more than people who always fly coach.

We are smiling from the moment we board. I arrange our business-class pods; we are gushingly polite to the attendants. It's obvious that we like each other and are happy to be traveling together. As soon as we get our beverages (in glasses!), we toast my sister and brother-in-law, who are paying for our business-class trip to Zurich.

Dignitas's office is in Zurich, and that's where we're headed. Dignitas is a Swiss nonprofit organization offering accompanied suicide. For the last twenty-two years, Dignitas has been the only place to go if you are an American citizen who wants to die and if you are not certifiably terminally ill with no more than six months to live. This is the current standard in the United States, even in the nine right-to-die states plus the District of Columbia, about which many older or chronically ill Americans harbor end-of-life fantasies and which I researched, at Brian's direction, until we discovered that the only place in the world for painless, peaceful, and legal suicide is Dignitas, in the suburbs of Zurich.

My sister had cried with me since the second appointment with the neurologist, when it took the doctor less than an hour to give Brian a mental-status exam and inform us that Brian almost certainly had Alzheimer's and had probably had it for several years, judging by his high IQ, his struggles with balance and proprioception, and his poor performance on the exam. It took Brian less than a week to decide that the "long goodbye" of Alzheimer's was not for him and less than a week for me to find Dignitas, at the end of several long Google paths. From summer to winter, my sister, Ellen, who loves me and loved Brian, did her best not to make suggestions, not to offer "if onlys," not to say that maybe Brian's Alzheimer's wouldn't be too bad or would progress very slowly, not to cry when I wasn't crying, and not to pour out her own grief at the loss of one of her favorite people and our compatible foursome. (When they met for the first time, fourteen years ago, Brian went into Ellen's kitchen with his winning ways and said, I really love your sister. My sister didn't turn around. She said, Hurt her and I will kill you.) Ellen called me early one morning in December, when we were pretty sure that we'd cleared the hurdles for Dignitas, and said, Just tell me what you need. I said, reluctantly, Twenty thousand, and my big sister said, Here's a check for thirty. We ended up spending every penny of it, between a couple of last big fishing trips for Brian, his not working, my not working, our eating out all the time, sometimes lunch and dinner, at the nicest restaurants in New Haven. We spent it on what was to be our last joint birthday celebration, and on four nights in the five-star hotel in Zurich and the car services and the tours of Zurich and my friend flying to and from Zurich to keep me company on the flight home, on whatever makes bad months bearable, plus the cost of Dignitas itself (around ten thousand dollars all in).

In our Swissair pods, Brian and I toast each other, and we say, *Here's to you,* a little hesitantly, instead of what we usually say, *Cent'anni* ("May we have a hundred years," a very Italian toast). There is no *Cent'anni* for us; we won't make it to our thirteenth wedding anniversary.

We lean closer to each other and then we pull back, each of us fussing with our shoes and carry-ons, each of us opening our little gift bags from the airline and pulling out the socks (yes) and the eye masks (never) and the tiny toothpastes and tiny toothbrushes, which we persist in believing will delight the grandchildren, which they never do.

It is all nearly normal, like so much that we've done these last few years, like the flight itself and everything that precedes it—the trip to the airport, the TSA (our petty but deep pleasure at having TSA PreCheck, noting the much longer, shoes-off lines to the left of us), the pretty good meal at JFK. It all seems normal, except that I still remember how different it was to be together, to be with Brian, three years ago, when I didn't hold my breath from the time he went off to the newsstand until he came back. From the outside, or some kind of inside (the one where I too have no memory of how we used to live our actual life), it is nearly normal.

For the trip to JFK, we didn't use Arnold, the guy who always drives our car to the airport and returns it to our driveway. Arnold's been driving us, and our kids and grandkids, for six years, and he has shared with us all about his love of motorcycles, his sobriety, and his wife's health issues, to balance, I think, all the information he has about us, whether he's wanted it or not. I could not bear to lie to Arnold about where we are going and I cannot bear to tell him the truth and I could not come up with a half-truth (the favorite technique of serious liars) about why we are going to Zurich in late January.

For the skiing? For the ice fishing? For the Chagall windows in Fraumünster Church? I was afraid that Arnold would watch us sympathetically in the rearview mirror, and I could not bear it, for Brian's pride and my general soft-boiledness, and just as I could not bear any harshness at all, I didn't think I could take kindness, either. I wanted absolutely nothing, a blanket of indifference, and that was exactly what we got from the driver of our local limo service. He spoke once in the two-and-a-half-hour drive. Perfect.

At JFK, we stood mid–Terminal 4 and agreed on the restaurant, nicer than Shake Shack (which I love and Brian does not) but not as nice as the Palm steakhouse, which seems insanely high-priced, but as I'm writing this, I remember that we did go to the Palm, after all, because . . . obviously.

Brian ordered everything he wanted—and, it seemed to me, everything that anyone can imagine ordering—at the Palm steakhouse at JFK, except vodka on the rocks, which he had been mentioning wanting from time to time for the last year or so.

At the Palm, Brian ordered onion rings and a rare rib eye with a side of hash browns and a Caesar salad and garlic toast and he would have ordered a shrimp cocktail, except that I whispered, like the circa-1953 stage Jewish wife I seem to have become, missing only my home perm and rickrack-trimmed apron: Really? Shrimp in a steak place, in an airport? Brian shrugged, to say: I'm not that excited about airport shrimp anyway and, also, what's the worst that could happen? I could have a bite, and it's meh, and then I wouldn't eat it. Waste of money, so what? I could *die* from bad shrimp, and wouldn't that save us all a lot of trouble? Or I could get food poisoning and have to miss the flight. At this, he folded the menu and looked at me the way he often did now, with resigned understanding, fatigue, a little worn humor.

I teared up all through dinner, with Brian occasionally patting my hand. I kept crying because I loved him and his appetites and all the sensuality and good humor and heat-seeking that went with them.

Sorry I Missed Your Call

For a little while, in 2007, Brian and I were bicoastal. I worked in L.A. on a short-lived TV show. He flew in from Hartford, right after work, every two weeks, took a quick nap in my office on Friday night, and woke up to have dinner with me and whoever was still around. He read multiple drafts of each week's show and watched the scenes when he could. He'd find a corner to sit in and take note of everything—costume, makeup, rehearsal, petty disagreements. He loved each surreal and complex part of shooting a show. One weekend, Brian woke up early and came back with an inflatable raft. He asked me to make sandwiches and drove us to the set in Burbank. He chatted up the security guard, who waved us in. We spent most of the day in and around a real pool, ate a real lunch, and lounged in the sun in our beautiful fake world.

When we left, Brian handed the security guard the bottle of white wine he'd chilled for him in the pool.

Two years ago, I gave Brian a new script of mine to read, and my husband, my cheerleader, TV-lover, inveterate script-reader, the man who half-hoped we'd wind up in Silver Lake and not Stony Creek, Connecticut, didn't read it. In the years we were together, Brian read everything I'd ever written, within days of my finishing. After a week, I asked about the TV script. Brian said that he hadn't gotten around to it. He sounded a little puzzled. Weeks went by and he didn't mention it. I steeled myself and asked him about it again and he said, with no chagrin and not much interest, that the format was too difficult to follow. He left it lying on the bedroom floor, until I took it back to my office.

Sunday, January 26, 2020, Zurich

At the JFK Palm, we ate and tipped well and then found our way to the Swissair lounge, which had been moved temporarily to the very distant lounge of Emirates Airline, where the female staff at the front desk combined brisk efficiency with an unmistakable nod to deference (an actual repeated head-duck) in their dealings with Brian. I got a bland sideways smile. I handled the tickets and I handled the passports and still, the longer we stood there, the more what-else-can-I do-for-you-Mr.-Ameche there was. Nothing comparable came my way. Brian did not mind. Even I didn't mind. Patriarchy, and my handsome husband, whaddayagonnado?

The lounge was clean and there was a lot of fruit and all sorts of buffet dishes—proper Middle Eastern, Italian-ish, French-ish—and a bustling bar. Brian snagged a big ball of falafel as we got settled. It wasn't stealing, of course, but I didn't think it was polite to reach out with your big fingers into the pile, when there were silver tongs, tiny forks, small plates, and matching small three-ply paper cocktail napkins waiting. Brian didn't care if it was rude, and the not caring wasn't a function of Alzheimer's. He had never cared.

We each have things we do that the other person finds faintly shocking. At home, I go outside to get the newspaper in what I call my pajamas—a ratty T-shirt and a pair of boxer shorts from college, rather than some fetching pink-piped set. We have neighbors. People can and do see me. I don't care. Brian was always, truly, appalled. He thought it was low-rent and, although he would never use the word, slatternly. (After the neurologist's appointment, he said, Why confuse people? Why make them think there are *two* people with Alzheimer's in the house? And we did both laugh and I still dash out of the house on Sunday mornings.) We are, my daughter the psychologist tells me, people with traces of mild sociopathy. I don't disagree.

Brian scouted the lounge for a satisfactory pair of arm-chairs and dove into the New York and London *Times*es. I don't know what reading the papers means to him anymore: politics, a bit of sports news (a football player at Yale in his day, he refuses to watch college football now, upset at the lack of care for the players, but he still keeps track of which teams are doing what). Some tidbits about real estate or architec-ture or design used to catch his eye, from his forty years as an architect. He never comments anymore. He used to read me several paragraphs at a clip about things that struck him, and even more, he loved for me to read articles to him while he drove. I never read aloud to him enough to suit him, but I

once did almost the entire *Sunday Review* while we pursued an
unlikely five-star BBQ place on the other side of Connecticut. When I faltered on the last Op-Ed piece, he said, "Finish
strong, darling."

Brian folded up the newspapers to bring on the plane and
then thought better of it. There was a whole style of planning, of near-hoarding of favorite things, of anticipating his
own needs, which has been his way since we met. He never
got into his car, from April to November, without making sure
he had at least one of his lesser fishing rods and some flies in
the trunk. He never left a restaurant without fistfuls of mints,
to put in his nightstand, candy jar, and glove compartment.
On this trip, he's done. I give him a wad of Swiss francs. He
knows where his medications are, plus his little vial of Viagra.
If he doesn't have it, he doesn't need it. If I'm not carrying it,
it's not important.

We take every little Swissair giveaway, for no reason, and we
hang on to our carry-on bags. I have insisted that we don't
bring proper suitcases, because I will not lug home a large
suitcase full of clothes he will never wear and medicines he
will never take—while packing, Brian shook a bottle of ten
Viagra at me like a maraca and said, This is worth something.

I won't dump his clothes at the Swiss version of Goodwill
and leave his meds for the cleaning staff. Basically, I just won't
deal with it, with "after." After Brian has died and I have to
leave him, my goal is to get myself on a plane with my friend
who has offered to accompany me home. Then my daughter
Sarah will meet me at the airport and Sarah and I will be met

by my daughter Caitlin and the two of them will say good night to me and my fantasy is that I will fall into my bed and not get up for two weeks. This is absolutely not what happens. We have brought our crappiest carry-on bags, black briefcases that double as overnight bags from Brian's business-travel days. Brian and I both hate the thought of throwing away a nice suitcase. Sociopaths, maybe, and given to splurging, yes, but not people who can throw out a barely used, unscratched, two-hundred-fifty-dollar suitcase.

The Book Brothers

When we moved to a small Connecticut village in 2014, Brian was invited to join a men's book club. He was dubious because they seemed to prefer nonfiction and he did not, but he was pleased to be asked and he went regularly. He suggested a novel whenever it was his turn to suggest. They asked him why he wanted to be in their book club and he said, I love a good read and I love intimacy. He was pleased that they looked shocked, and he felt that he'd announced himself properly. Once in a while, he has coffee on a weekend with one of the guys. He says the books are usually too simple ("I don't know. It's about some horse who overcomes obstacles") or sentimental ("Olympic team of rowers. They win") for him, but he enjoyed the group and the chatting before and after until two years ago, when almost everything about the book club began to irritate him.

I hear him grumbling when the emails come in: There are too many schedule changes; he doesn't know which house the meeting's at and they expect him to know by now which man lives where, so they don't always attach the address of the meeting. He goes to a meeting on the wrong night but he doesn't mind, because a few months earlier, a "book brother" showed up at our house a week early. Brian tells me that one of the men he really likes, with whom he'd had lunch a couple of years ago, is moving out of town. I encourage Brian to call him for a last lunch, but he says that it's too late, that the man has already moved away. One day, I look at Brian's phone (I often find myself looking at Brian's phone these last two years, but I pretend I don't) and I see an email from the man who I thought moved away, putting in his pitch for the book he'd like the group to read. He has moved about ten minutes farther away and is still very much in the book club.

This fall, Brian has gotten the book for his book club (meaning, I picked it up from our library, across the street) and talks to me about it with enthusiasm. But I can see that not only does the bookmark not advance, it goes backward, every couple of days, to the first ten pages. He doesn't go to the meeting and the book sits on his nightstand for months, even as we are packing for Zurich, because even when he sees it, it doesn't matter, or he has forgotten about it, and because I cannot bear to touch or even mention it.

Monday, January 27, 2020, Zurich

We land in Zurich and the hotel's car service takes us to the pretty hotel in the cobblestoned Old Town section. The city's warmer than we expect, and it's drizzling. The Widder is a bunch of old buildings pulled together into a posh hotel through oddly placed lifts and corridors, the kind of hotel we might choose for a holiday, although it has never occurred to either of us, ever, to go to Zurich. Every restaurant we pass is filled with couples, most of whom are apparently pairs of straight white men in business-ish clothes. Sometimes, they are foursomes. Occasionally, there is a businessman in his late sixties and a hot young thing in a silk minidress and strappy sandals (My God, I think, the cobblestones). Between Brian's trouble with proprioception this past year—gashed his hand, slipped off the front porch, tumbled backward off a picnic bench—and my new-for-Zurich terror that he will slip and fall on the wet cobblestones of Old Town and we will not be able to get ourselves to Dignitas, the cobblestones—and conversations about cobblestones—loom very large on this trip.

I feel shifty and out of place at the hotel's front desk. Brian wanders around, in and out of the lobby, and when I see him walk through a pair of swinging doors at the end of the hall while I am searching for our passports, my stomach hurts, as it does every time he leaves my sight. When he comes back a few minutes later, I've pulled myself together. Every time the concierge asks me a question, I fumble like a suspect. Why are we here? Would we like a map of all the stores on Bahnhofstrasse (Gucci, Fendi, Hublot, Cartier)? May they show me the bar and the library? I want to say to Brian that it reminds me a little of a hotel we loved in Amsterdam, but I am afraid that he won't remember the trip, the hotel. I am afraid that he won't but he will pretend that he does and I won't know if he does or he doesn't, which is awful, or I will know he doesn't, which is also awful, and I don't say anything, which is usually the choice I make now. We are both exhausted by the time we get to our room.

The room is hotel-pleasant and pretty, with floor-to-ceiling French windows, looking down on a bakery, a jewelry store. (Brian encourages me to go in and the stuff is lovely and he picks out a ring he thinks I'll like and I do like it and we're both pleased. He has gotten me some really ugly jewelry in the last three years, things that are so far from my taste that, if he were a different man, I'd think he was keeping a Seventies-boho, broke-ass mistress in Westville and gave me by mistake the enameled copper earrings and bangle he bought for her. The Zurich rings are beautiful, beaten gold and custom-made with small blue opals, like bits of night, and ten thousand dollars apiece. Brian and I smile politely and walk out. He says, I wanted you to have something . . . and I know he means to remember him by, and this is the last time we cry together, before Thursday.)

It's raining but couples are strolling into bars and the big, old-fashioned tea shop on the corner. We might have come for a holiday. I guess.

Back in our room, we stand in front of the big window for a few minutes, and I taste it again, the metallic tang of almost normal. If it was truly normal, we'd unpack and shower. That is, Brian would unpack. I would dick around and then shower and hope that he might unpack for me, which rarely happens. Then we'd get into bed and nap or make love (there's always a lot of Viagra to use up; the man stocked up on Viagra the way my mother hoarded canned goods—*just in case*) or we'd bundle ourselves out the door to the Moroccan restaurant in Paris where the chef would come rushing to greet us when he heard Brian's voice. (On our first visit and Brian's big order, he came out and looked at our table in surprise: Only the two of you? He laughed and then he brought Brian two more small tagines, because Brian hadn't yet tried the lamb or the pigeon.) The punkish headshop/barbershop in London where we'd always go right after landing, suitcase in hand, where Brian got the best haircut of his life in a shop so small, we were both high by the time we left it. This time, we stare out the window and we both sigh. We undress and crawl into bed. Brian sleeps for a couple of hours.

I worry, sometimes, that a better wife, certainly a different wife, would have said no, would have insisted on keeping her husband in this world until his body gave out. It seems to me that I'm doing the right thing, in supporting Brian in his decision, but it would feel better and easier if he could make all the arrangements himself and I could just be a dutiful duckling, following in his wake. Of course, if he could make all the arrangements himself, he wouldn't have Alzheimer's—and if he had wanted to make all the arrangements on his own, he wouldn't have been Brian. I walk this loop in my mind as I wake up and unpack.

I think of Susie Chang, my eminently sensible Tarot card reader (and if you think that it's absurd to find comfort in Tarot, I've got no argument for you), who uses the Crow deck to take a look at what might happen, or what I might wish to mitigate. My daughters appear, repeatedly, as two crows, or two lions, or two shields in front of me, and, again, if you think that this is the height of idiocy, I don't disagree. Turning over the Chariot card, in a last reading before Brian and I travel, Susie and I see a small crab in the corner. "This is your card," Susie Chang says. "You have to drive this chariot, you have to drive it with a hard shell, because otherwise it will crush you beneath the wheel." She says, "You cannot let go until it is over." I make an I-know-I-know noise. She taps the card and says, If you let go of the reins, it will crush you, and I burst into tears. Most of the time, I do feel like the little crab, armored and fragile.

I have brought nothing to Zurich but washed-out black and gray clothes and my everyday underwear. I will not be—as my mother would have said about other things—making an effort. I try to figure out which "fun" things we'll do in Zurich.

At home, we'd had a pretty good time making a list of a dozen things, including the best restaurants of Zurich. In the end we do get to the Chagall windows, a couple of walks down Bahnhofstrasse, Lake Zurich (There is Tina Turner's house, the guide says, and we wave. It seems to me that she has had a lovely, loving marriage to this Swiss guy, and I'm glad for her), and a not-bad Italian place around the corner. The whole trip, I can wear only yoga pants and one moth-eaten cardigan. Now that we're here, struggling to pull ourselves together to go down for dinner, I think that if we can show up for breakfast, smile at the concierge, take the tour of Lake Zurich that we've already booked, and visit those famous Chagall stained-glass windows, since one of Brian's hobbies is making stained glass, we will have done a great job—and filled the time from Monday to Thursday morning.

Our first night, we do manage to go down to the Widder's Michelin-starred restaurant, but it's confusing to both of us. There's no water and no bread. The waiter seems more like a guy trying to finish his dissertation, waiting for us to leave his carrel.

"You know tapas?" the waiter says, and I say that we do indeed know tapas.

"So, this is our version of tapas," he says, and hands us the menu, which lists three prawns for fifty dollars, a small venison sausage for forty. On the next table, we see one meatball and one sliced mushroom in a spoonful of beef broth. Brian and I stare at the meatball and the menu and the waiter stands perfectly still and we order chicken sandwiches from the bar. I'm too mad to order a twenty-two-dollar Aperol spritz. The fries are excellent.

The Provisional Green Light

We have a day to fill before our first interview with Dr. G., the Swiss doctor from Dignitas who will conduct two interviews with Brian, one Monday and one Wednesday, before our appointment at the Dignitas apartment on Thursday. We'd been informed, in our last phone call with our Dignitas contact person, Heidi, who has now revealed her actual name to us (S.), that we're "on our way to the provisional green light," and then we got the more-official email, stating that we had now received the provisional green light and a Swiss doctor would write the prescription for the sodium pentobarbital that Brian would drink for his "accompanied suicide" in the Dignitas apartment. So, if Brian does as well as expected in the interviews, with Dr. G. checking on Brian's discernment and determination, we'll get the full green light on Wednesday and go to the Dignitas apartment on Thursday. (As my sister said, It's like you do everything you possibly can to get your kid into Harvard and when you do, they kill him. Ellen was horrified it came out of her mouth and I was horrified to hear it, but she wasn't wrong.)

I never pushed back with Dignitas in any way. I hadn't complained when our phone interviews at home in the fall were regularly delayed and we were notified a half hour later, by email ("They're *Swiss*," I said. "How can they be late? How can they be late, again?"), even though Brian and I were sitting in the kitchen, unbearably tense, bagels put aside so as not to make any untoward noises, waiting for the phone to ring, waiting to put Brian on speakerphone so that if they asked something important to which he could not find the answer, I could write it down in the notebook in front of us and he could then answer. This only happened once, when S. asked him why he wanted to end his life and he paused, not because he didn't know the answer but because he'd forgotten the word for Alzheimer's. Sometimes he said *Anheuser*, as in Anheuser-Busch, maker of adequate beer, and sometimes he said *Arthritis*. By the time we leave home for Zurich, he's forgetting the names of our grandchildren and mixing up the dates of all kinds of things, he can't find his way through the grocery store, but he always remembers the name of his disease.

On the phone call with S., I wrote ALZHEIMERS, as neatly as I could with a shaking hand, in giant letters. Brian nodded to me and cleared his throat, as if it's just that he was moved by the gravity of the question, and then he answers thoughtfully: I don't want to end my life, he said, but I'd rather end it while I am still myself, rather than become less and less of a person.

This is the call we have been working toward since August, five months, when it became clear that Dignitas was Brian's best choice and probably, really, his only one.

We might have gotten there sooner had it not been for the neurologist who wrote in the lab report for Brian's MRI that she was ordering it because of a "major depressive episode." This was easy to write and not true, and if she had been a little more diligent or accurate, we might have been accepted by Dignitas in September and, in fact, we would not have been ready. By December, when S. told us that we could go forward with the process, that we could come to Zurich in January, the real thing was upon us, the world without Brian in it, the world going on without him, me alone and him in the earth or in the stars but not next to me. After we thanked S. one more time, we hung up, weeping in each other's arms, and, without speaking, went right up to bed for a nap at 11 A.M.

Monday, January 27, 2020, Zurich

According to Dignitas data, 70 percent of the people who get the provisional green light never contact Dignitas again; the reassurance, the insurance, is all they need. That was not us. In early December, we were still hoping for the green light. We'd received an email that the Dignitas office would be closed from December 21 to January 6. It also said that we'd sent them the wrong form for Brian's birth certificate and our appointments in Zurich could not, would not, be scheduled until those papers were received. S. attached a list of recommended hotels, all of them sounding pleasant enough, several of them very chalet-like, with lots of gingerbread and overlooking Lake Zurich.

But Brian didn't want to take healthy hikes around the lake. He wanted to be in the center of the city, in either the oldest or the most modern part, as he always does. He told me to get some other hotel suggestions. He said, Just google some places and show me, and we began our virtual tour of Zurich, a cold German Swiss city famous for chocolate, some good fishing in the spring, holding on to the bank deposits that persecuted Jews made during World War II and not giving back a franc or a painting until 2000, and one good restaurant overlooking the famous Chagall windows.

(Short version: When we do get to Zurich, the windows are nice. The Fraumünster Church offered the commission to Chagall in the Seventies, when he was eighty years old. He finished the five windows in three years: Jacob wrestling with the Angel. The End of Days—angel with trumpet. Giant Crucifixion scene. I love Chagall and these bored me to fucking tears. Brian looked and looked, checking out the paint colors, the lines, and the soldering, and then we both turned away in the shadowy sacristy. We didn't care and we weren't moved. We had a better time in the tea shop afterward, eating exceptional, perfect cakes of red velvet topped with wobbling red gelatin and, on top of that, thin chocolate domes like bonnets. That, we could get behind. Fifteen minutes for the windows, one hour for the pastries.)

July 2019

The Blue Notebooks

I'm hoping the neurologist we've made the appointment with will have an explanation for the past few years of things that Brian's done that have puzzled me or hurt me and constantly worried me: After complaining about his phone and the calendar on the phone, Brian has started carrying a six-page paper calendar all over the house, from room to room, as my grandmother used to carry her ancient plastic handbag. When I say, We don't need the calendar, he bristles. When I remind him that we have a large whiteboard calendar in the kitchen for coordinating doctor's appointments, social engagements, and that, at his request, I've filled in a lot of squares with his appointments and mine, he says, I never look at that thing.

When I say, hoping for a fun evening like we used to have (for two working adults, we took in a lot of movies and a lot of popcorn), Let's go to the movies tonight or tomorrow, he gets up, searches for his paper calendar, and comes back to me, studying it hard, although there's always a seven o'clock movie at the 12-plex five minutes away and we have neither children at home nor a dog. He brandishes the calendar every time we talk about any coming event, including getting takeout. I see him writing things down, in his new jagged handwriting.

Several years ago, we started keeping a notebook "to help our communication." I liked the idea more than Brian did but eventually he took to it, using it to let me know that he'd gone for a walk, or we needed toilet paper, or he was out running errands. The notebook also made it easier for him not to use his phone, and he liked that a lot. The notebooks had begun, when we first married, with my leaving a scrap of paper on the kitchen counter, anchored by a saltshaker. It might say: *Your mother called* or *Dinner with So-and-So Saturday night.* Brian found this unsatisfactory—probably slipshod, certainly unserious—and so he asked for a notebook. A few years ago, each notebook began to have very specific things wrong with it: too big, too small, the days not dated, the hours not noted. I made every single change (not always nicely) and eventually we settled on a series of navy-blue spiral notebooks and I learned to put the day and the date at the top of every page, in large letters. I learned to list things separately and clearly and I learned that being clever or cute (drawings, stickers, questions) was not only a waste of time but annoying to him. We went through dozens of those navy-blue notebooks, and by the time we went to Zurich, it was one of the few methods of communication that did not fail us regularly.

I have them still.

My tone in correspondence with Dignitas was always restrained pleading, plus a little humor, to show that we would not be difficult, and a thread of please-note-my-very-Swiss-attention-to-detail. I have become as English as possible (you cannot have Jewish *geshrei*-ing and Italian *agitarsi* with the Swiss German, is what I believe). Every email I send them has either the words *quite* or *a bit* or *perhaps* and usually all three. I want to demonstrate patience, clarity, and some sort of appealing and demure stoicism.

> We are a bit concerned that since our contact person is not in the office this week, we will receive no information about planning until after January 6.
>
> That does feel to us like a long time before we can even begin to plan.

When you write that our contact person "will be in touch as soon as possible," what is that time frame, please?

Thank you for all of your help.

Brian Ameche and Amy Bloom

Von: Amy Bloom
Gesendet: Dienstag, 17. Dezember 2019 15:44
An: Dignitas
Betreff: Birth certificate received

Dear Mrs. Bloom, Dear Mr. Ameche,

Your contact person will get back to you as soon as possible, latest after our holidays on 06 January 2020.

Your sincerely, Team DIGNITAS

DIGNITAS
Menschenwürdig leben
Menschenwürdig sterben

Monday Evening, January 27, 2020, Zurich

I hope to be patient, stoic, and demure with Dr. G., when he comes to our hotel. He's phoned me twice and moved our interview twice and we are now, oddly, settled on Monday at 10 P.M. The late hour makes it seem shadier and more important. I worry that Dr. G. will stop at the front desk and they will see that he's here to interview Brian, to give him the medical green light for his appointment on Thursday—and someone, some well-meaning, life-affirming bellhop or night manager, will stop us. I wonder if I should loiter in the lobby to keep this from happening. Brian says I should do nothing of the kind. I try to figure out what kind of answers Brian will need to give Dr. G. and how I should behave. I put on my black shirt and my black cardigan and look in the mirror. The Swiss seem quite conservative, so this might be the right note to strike. I want to demonstrate support, of the right kind, whatever that may be. Fortunately, I didn't marry for money, and no matter how hard the Swiss authorities dig, it will be clear that I do not have "a financial interest or benefit" for marrying Brian or for supporting his ending his life. Do they look for signs of true brokenheartedness and not just mere resignation? This "evidence of financial interest or benefit" is, as it turns out, the loophole on which all of Dignitas's services depend. Swiss law says, explicitly, that it is illegal to assist or encourage a suicide if you have a clear financial interest; the law says "selfish interests," which seem to me to cover more than cash in the event of the person's death. However, if you do *not*, you can assist someone in ending their life—and that's how Dignitas has done it for three thousand people, so far.

September 2005, Durham, Connecticut

How We Met

B rian and I fell in love the way some middle-aged people in unhappy partnerships and in small towns do: liberal Democrats in a Republican town, ethnic types in a town full of Northern Europeans, opinionated loudmouths, and people who were willing to man the Durham Democrats Hot Dog Stand (hot dogs and cider) every September at the fair. I overlooked his bad haircut and aviator glasses. I'm sure he had to overlook my lack of interest in sports and my impatience (Brian could talk about a plastic gazebo or additional parking at the library for hours). We had been walking together, since our partners were not walkers, and talking together in public, at our local Democrats breakfast club, and then, suddenly, talking in private. He said, I was a three-sport captain in high school, and I laughed. He said, It would have been four sports but you can't do lacrosse *and* baseball. Is that right, I said, and he took my hand. He said, What's your family like? I said, Jews from New York. You? He said, Well, we're a football family. We have three Heisman trophies in my family. I said, What's a Heisman, and he kissed me. I kissed him back and, sensibly, we avoided each other for the next year. After a year, and some martinis in New Haven at the end of the day, he asked me to take a walk with him.

He said, I'm not stupid. I know how this will end. You'll tell me we should not do this to the people we love, or I'll tell you, and we will go back to our lives, where we should be. And I will never get over this. Or, we blow up our lives and be together.

I just want to say this, he said, before we walk back to our cars. I know who you could be with. Someone rich, someone fancy, some guy your sister finds for you. But I know who you should be with. You should be with a guy who doesn't mind that you're smarter than he is, who doesn't mind that most of the time, you'll be the main event. You need to be with a guy who supports how hard you work and who'll bring you a cup of coffee late at night. I don't know if I can be that guy, he said, tears in his eyes, but I'd like a shot.

We married.

Monday Evening Continued, January 27, 2020, Zurich

As I understand it, Dr. G. is both our guide through the process and a possible speed bump. Brian's clear on everything except the day and date, and I make the decision that the day and the date cannot be important because drilling him on it frightens us and wears us out. The friend-of-a-friend who'd brought her father with brain cancer to Dignitas told me that it was very important that Brian open the hotel room door, showing that he's in charge of the process. I tell Brian this and he nods but I can tell he's not going to jump up at the first knock. Brian is not someone who rushes (period) to host, at any gathering we've ever had. He loves being the guest and he makes up for it by doing a ton of dishes after. I don't know how to make sure he answers the door or even if it's important. I just keep saying: The doctor's gonna knock on our hotel room door. (I'm also worried about etiquette. Will the doctor expect a cup of tea? Does he look like the Grim Reaper? No and no.)

The doctor does knock on the door and I almost scream.

Brian strolls over to the door and is his most amiable and pleasant, Brian self. (We used to say that Brian could talk to anyone. He could make small talk with a stump and, in the end, that stump would be hugging Brian goodbye, thanking him for a great evening, and inviting us all to the next stump get-together.)

Dr. G. is a small man with large, lovely, mournful eyes. We all shake hands and Brian and Dr. G. sit across from each other. I ask Dr. G. if I can stay for the conversation and he looks surprised. He says, gently, that of course I should stay, as this all concerns me, as well. I begin crying and both men look at me kindly. I pour myself a glass of water. Dr. G. ("Moishe," he says. That's my father's name, and I feel lightly blessed somehow and I know that I have lost my mind) asks about our flight. He mentions, complaining lightly, just *en passant*, in what I can only describe as the Jewish fashion of complaining while assuring us, at the beginning and end of each sentence, that he is certainly not complaining, that he had to come so late at night because he was at a concert in the city and it was most convenient, coming after the concert, because he lives by the lake and doesn't come into town every day but since we chose to stay in the Old Town, he had to make a special trip just to see us—not that he's complaining. I beg him to take a glass of water and he does, probably so I'll stop crying. He opens a folder and says to Brian, After I read your application, I knew I would see you, but I didn't think it would be this soon. Brian says, It's not a big window. I mean, no one knows how long they have, how much time they have, to make this choice. Dr. G. looks like he might argue but instead he says, You're absolutely right.

He says that he began helping Dignitas (he is an ophthal-mologist) after his father's death from Alzheimer's, which was long and painful, in every way. He says that Dignitas uses eight doctors and they are all pretty busy. I worry that he will men-tion again how much extra time it takes to schlep from the lake into the city, but he doesn't. He says to Brian, I will ask you several times, many times, if you are sure that this is what you wish to do and I want you to understand that at any time, at any time between now and the final act, you are free to change your mind and not do this. I hope you will not do this, he says softly, and Brian nods. So, Dr. G. says, Are you sure that you wish to end your life on Thursday? Brian says that he is sure. I start crying again and, thank God, both men ignore me again. Dr. G. smiles and nods.

It seems to me, he says pleasantly, holding up the folder, you don't believe in anything, Mr. Ameche. Brian laughs and says, I believe in a lot of things, but religion and the afterlife are not among them. Well, Dr. G. says, chuckling, you'll find out before I will. Let me know. Brian smiles.

Dr. G.'s tone changes. Let me tell you what will happen: You will arrive at our apartment building in the suburbs of Zurich, in the morning, by 10 A.M. Do not be late. You will be greeted by two people from Dignitas. They will invite you in. You can take your time, he says. There will be no rushing. He looks at me, as if he can tell that I am the rushing sort, and I want to assure him that every minute of our time in Zurich is me trying to push back the clock.

There is some paperwork. There are chocolates. They will give you an anti-emetic, he says, so you will not vomit. You have up to an hour after that to make your choice about drinking the drink. If you need more time, they will administer the anti-emetic again. And again, you will have about an hour after that to drink the drink. After you drink it—it is a little bitter, he says, and I wonder how he knows. After you drink it, you will fall into a light sleep, then a deep sleep. Then it will be over. Mrs. Ameche, you can sit with him for a long time. (I'm glad he calls me Mrs. Ameche. I know Brian always gets a kick out of that.)

Brian nods attentively. Dr. G. says, At any time in this process, you may change your mind. Right now, or Thursday morning. No one will be surprised or distressed. We will all be glad for you. (I don't know why this would be. Perhaps I would be glad, too, but only if it meant the spell was broken and my whole husband was returned to me and to himself and these last years turned out to have been just a terrible test, one poisoned apple after another, to prove that my darling deserves the life he had before.) Brian shakes his head.

"I know what I'm doing," he says. "This is the right thing for me."

Dr. G. nods. "I see that," he says. "But I will keep asking."

Brian and I sit back down, after he's gone. I say that Dr. G. seemed nice and Brian agrees. Brian says, It's going okay, and I agree. We sleep side by side, fingertips touching.

Babu, King of Castles

With every one of our little girls, our granddaughters (Brian never thought, for one minute, that he should have had children. "I'm the baby," he said cheerfully), Brian became a better and better grandfather, the best Babu. "I feel like I robbed a bank," he often said. "Never had kids and went straight to grandchildren. How lucky am I?" With every little girl, there was a phase, between two and four, when he was the Lego god, the Lord of the Towers and King of Castles, and we have pictures of each of them standing on Brian's desk or coffee table, taller than he is, pointing proudly to the stack of blocks towering above them. Brian praised anything that seemed to show architectural or engineering skills: She copied the picture perfectly! Look how stable that is—she built a decent foundation! See how she put all the blue ones on one corner of the building envelope? I did a building like that.

When each girl got a little older and expressed interest in the more elaborate Legos, Brian would be at the kitchen table, attaching hard pink bouquets to tiny green stems, building and decorating a pastel brick wall with elaborate mosaics, hitching cellphone-size lilac RVs to tiny cars, while the little girl waited happily, occasionally handing him a piece of plastic or sharing some chocolate. (A visiting cousin found the bowl of candy on Brian's nightstand and said, Oh, Uncle Brian is the luckiest man in the world. The granddaughters shrugged, happy to be in the know, happy to be the special people who could stick their hands right into Babu's Candy Jar in the pantry and get nothing but a knowing wink from Babu, who could be counted on to turn his broad back, to hide them from their parents.)

Tuesday, January 28, 2020, Zurich

We walk around, exploring the fancy shops on Bahnhof-strasse, and we walk down to Lake Zurich again. We walk back. We can't bring ourselves to go into the shops or browse the way we normally would. (We once spent a joyful half hour in an insanely expensive men's clothing store in Chicago, just so Brian could try on dark-blue fedoras and Missoni mufflers and cashmere pullovers.) There's a toy store near the hotel and we concentrate on that. I want to bring all the granddaughters something from Zurich. We get the twins, Eden and Ivy, a snow globe of two bunnies, even though I don't like getting them gifts to share; there is only one snow globe, and it suddenly seems that there will not be a single decent gift in all of Zurich for me to bring back.

Our cover story is: Nana and Babu went on a vacation to Europe. While there, Babu died of a disease in his brain.

I've talked this over, a dozen times, with my therapist, Wayne. When the pace of my worrying and complaining about Brian became nonstop, a friend gave me a referral to Wayne, a psychiatrist—a man I'd met forty years earlier when I was a graduate student and he was striding Yale's halls like a psychoanalytic god. I called him, introduced myself, said we'd met before; he clearly didn't remember me and then I burst into tears. I said, I hope you can help me. I want to kill my husband, and I kept on crying. He said, You want to kill him because you love him, and I said, You are so right. Wayne, as far as I am concerned, saved me before and after this trip to Zurich, and in the end, he saved Brian, too.

Wayne used to treat children as well as adults. I've talked over what to say about Babu and his death, with Wayne and with my children, the parents of our four gorgeous little girls, Brian's adoring pack. Wayne says, again and again, simplest is best, and none of this is untrue. I've told my children that if they wish to go another way with his story, if there is another approach they wish to take, I will respect that. None of us conclude that getting into the right to die and how we came to that and that I sat with their beloved Babu while he passed from life to death and let him and why I let him—with an eleven-year-old, two six-year-olds, and a two-year-old—will be helpful. They will all miss him terribly and I'm pretty sure that none of them have perceived any malfunction in him. Yet I know that if we were not going to Dignitas now, soon they would be sad and relieved for his life to come to its end, and this way they are just heartbroken. It matters to Brian and to me that they will remember him as their loving, fun, goofy, candy-sharing, soft-touch Babu. I figure that when each of them gets to be old enough, if they want to, they will read this book and his lovely little notes written to each of them, all of which begin: *I wish I could stay longer.* And when they are teenagers, they may be angry that we lied to them, and that will be okay. This is the best we can do.

Wednesday, January 29, 2020, Zurich

We shop, we go to dinner, we meet my oldest friend, who has flown in just to fly home with me, when I have to travel without Brian. Other people, including all of my children, volunteered to come. My son said, If you don't want me there while the two of you are there, I'll just meet you in Zurich Airport on Thursday and fly home with you. Some people offered quickly and then withdrew their offers a little later, when they contemplated the actual trip. My oldest friend called and said, Tell me what you need, and I did tell her, on speakerphone, so Brian could also have his say. We don't need much while we're there, I tell her. Brian nods and he shouts, Thanks, darling! before we hang up. I text her later that I expect that I will not be functioning very well at Zurich Airport on the way home and her only job is to get me on the plane and home to Newark Airport, without any major fuckups. She says, I can do that, and she does.

We have one more day to fill. We take walks—I photo-
graph the intersections so we won't get lost, and every time
I hold up my phone, Brian walks on and says, We'll be fine.
We chat listlessly. I find an index card in my bag when I get
home: *January 29, agony and tedium.* We sleep after every meal.
When Brian wakes up, we read some poetry off my phone:
Brian's man, John Ciardi, his girl Szymborska; and I read my
Janes, Hirshfield and Kenyon. I read them to myself because
I cannot read them aloud and I can't even look at the line *Let
the envious gods take back what they can* from my favorite Hirshfield
poem because, boy, they've shown me, those envious gods,
haven't they just? Brian says he wants to take a walk and puts
on his jacket. I grab my sweater and my notebook, where I
wrote down Dr. G.'s suggestion for the best routes. I'm like a
people-pleasing agoraphobic here in Zurich; the idea of going
beyond the tea shop on the corner terrifies me and I actively
wish to conceal this fact from Brian. I've only become an anxious person in the last few months, and my coping and deflect-
ing mechanisms are not polished.

   We can't even play gin. We can't read. I would like to have
some heartfelt, leaf-shaking conversations, the way I imagine
some people get to, at the end of life. (I imagine this despite
having sat at multiple deathbeds, at which there definitely were
no last-minute confessions, assertions, or expressions of deep
feeling. The people dying were often in pain and exhausted or
heavily medicated. My father patted my hand and thought I
was my mother. My mother grabbed my arm and said, Jesus,
honey, do something about the pain. As my old man used to
say, frequently, regarding my expectations: the triumph of
hope over experience.)

PART II

End of Life

It's amazing to me that people said to me, "Well, why go to Switzerland? I mean, why not Oregon or Colorado or Hawaii or Vermont? There are right-to-die laws in those states." (That some people said this to me right before—and right *after*—my husband died was more than amazing.) The right-to-die (physician-assisted dying) laws in California, Colorado, Oregon, Vermont, Montana (as a result of a 2009 State Supreme Court decision), District of Columbia, New Jersey, Maine, Hawaii, and Washington require that you be or become a resident of that state (sometimes quick and easy, not always) in order to pursue your physician-assisted suicide and also—consistently—that you are mentally competent, medically assessed as having only six months to live, and can express your wish to die, usually three times, twice orally and once in writing, to two local physicians.

These laws are pretty much the same and they are intentionally eye-of-the-needle. Practically speaking, you have to be damn close to death's door to get a doctor to swear that you'll be dead in six months. You have two physician interviews, some days apart, in which you assert that you are not psychotic or suicidal or depressed and hope the doctors agree with you. You have to be able to swallow what the doctor prescribes, without any assistance. Will the doctor be thoughtful enough to give you a powder that dissolves into a bitter but easy-to-drink four ounces? In some states, you have to be able to get yourself into a pharmacy to purchase your lethal prescription, because assisting you in any way is illegal. I'm not sure how much enforcement of this clause there is.

Choosing to die and being able to act independently while terminally ill is a deliberately narrow opening. Many people can't get through it. They can't swallow well enough. They can't talk well enough. They can't hold the glass or mix the drink on their own. (Helping someone hold the glass is a crime in most of America.)

People who do wish to end their lives and shorten their period of great suffering and loss—those people are out of luck in the United States of America.

March 2019, Stony Creek, Connecticut

Something Sudden and Slow

I was lucky—I guess—that Brian got worried about his memory loss after he had hip surgery and was willing to get tested, mostly because he thought and hoped his poor memory might be just a bad reaction to the anesthesia used for the hip implant in March. I'd gotten worried about his memory and balance a couple of years earlier, and since he was now worried, I could say I was worried, too.

Still, his memory loss felt sudden: names disappearing, repetition, information turned upside down, appointments and medications scrambled. Suddenly, it seemed, we argued endlessly about everything.

After admiring his hip-replacement handiwork at the post-op checkup, Brian's excellent surgeon, Dr. Hipandknee, said, That does happen—memory loss, post-operative cognitive decline, reaction to anesthesia. He said he didn't think that Brian was the kind of patient to whom it would happen: healthy and with no heart problems. But faced with Brian's nonstop complaints threatening to dampen our post-surgery walk-across-the-room celebration, Dr. Hipandknee added that he had had a few patients who got foggy and memory-impaired after that kind of anesthesia and he said, in the confident manner of excellent surgeons who know that the operation has been a slam-dunk success, It'll pass, give it six weeks.

In those six weeks, Brian's short-term memory got a little better but he retreated in other ways. A gregarious man, he didn't want to see friends, except to fish. He now talked only about the past, his childhood and football. I could not steer him to any other subjects. In the evenings, I said—because I didn't know any better—that maybe we could talk about our life now, as it's going on, him and me and his retirement and the kids and the grandchildren and our friends, and he said, Sure, but we didn't, and the evenings were hours of television.

One spring morning, I'd been weeping because Brian seemed so distant and, in that moment, weeping the harder because, although I could see that he was concerned and truly sorry he had upset me, I could also see that he didn't really know why I was upset, and reminding him of our long, point-less fight the day before wasn't helping. We still had the occasional Sunday-morning conversations that we'd always had and cherished: Somebody hurt somebody's feelings and some-body is owed an apology, which will be forthcoming sooner from me, later from him, but delivered by dinnertime. Brian was not immune to the lure of the I-didn't-say-it or if-I-said-it-I-didn't-mean-it approach, but one of the things I loved was his willingness to own up. There'd be a burst of anger, the black cloud would pass, and my husband would dig a little deeper and usually come up with a genuine apology (my favorite: "I'm sorry I was such a knucklehead"). The cloud didn't pass now; the apology was thin or weary or cold.

I could feel him through a glass and I was banging on it, screaming at him: Why is there a glass between us? Where did it come from? Take it down! And Brian looked at me with puzzled, irritated concern and said, in effect, What glass? And, Please, please stop complaining about this thing that isn't even there.

I called the neurologist and made an appointment. By the time we did get to see a neurologist, the urgent short-term memory-loss problem had receded, Brian was still talking only about the past, and we were left with the glass between us, and problems that were intractable, and multiplying.

Messages Not Received

By late 2016, I knew something was wrong. I began read-ing the Alzheimer's information and research websites and the caregiver blogs obsessively for a while, then not at all. I stopped reading them because I could not bear to know what it was that was wrong. Every page of every Alzheimer's website emphasizes what must be done to deal with the loss of cognitive function (the appointments, the cellphone, the driv-ing, and later the names, the hygiene, the missing chunks of personal history plus a highlights reel of the very distant past), but many of them focus, especially in the early, post-diagnosis days, on the way in which the person is still there, despite the losses. (*Not all doom and gloom,* as one says.) And some medical sites do tell you how it is when the person begins to fade away, as the neurons stop functioning, lose connections with other neurons, and die. Neurons connect, communicate, and repair, and that's what Alzheimer's destroys, connection within and without, first in the entorhinal cortex and hippocampus (the part of the brain devoted to memory) and then in the cerebral cortex (language, processing, and social behavior).

Those neurons, the brain's soldiers, march for years, from the time we're born, through the byways of the brain, setting actions into motion, rolling away boulders of all kinds, and then, with Alzheimer's, they're blocked by trees down at one end of the road, dangling wires at another. Over the years, the brain's soldiers—this well-trained and reliable army, which has done so much, on so many different terrains, gone high and low, swum, climbed, strolled, and marched to all the different destinations of the mind—begin to falter, long before outsiders can see the troubles. Eventually (five years on for some, three for others, ten for some), the obstacles cannot be overcome. Messages cannot be received. The soldiers cannot break through to new ground. Retreat is the only possible path and you'd be a fool to try to lure someone out, amid the heavy artillery. Alzheimer's for me is 1914, and a good day with Brian now is that famous Christmas truce, which was quite short and quite beautiful (German boys caroling to the English, calling out, "Merry Christmas, Englishmen," as they climbed out of the trenches; tobacco shared, souvenirs exchanged, rations shared, and prisoners swapped) and never repeated. Retreat makes sense, and it is agony for me and, I think, not much of anything now for Brian.

That steady loss, that steady unraveling, is sometimes paused but never stopped. The shape of the self is held together as well as can be, with the use of alternative pathways in the brain (Brian began addressing each of the granddaughters as "darling" or "little girl," and he referred to his book club only as "those guys") by the person suffering and with backup from the person helping, until none of it's enough and the vessel, some beautiful Egyptian jug of Nile clay and jute, begins to soften and drop its walls, but not sharply, only as if the straw is pulled out, stalk by stalk, and then it's not the jug it was, it can't hold a thing. It's a pile of clay and straw in the palm of your own hand.

Dignitas

Dignitas in 2020 has served more than three thousand people and has a rival, a competing organization, Pegasos, created by the brother of a doctor who left Dignitas. So now there are *two* places, in the entire world, where you can go to end your life painlessly if you are not suicidal, psychotic, or advanced in your dementia, and I'm glad of it, although my heart is with Dignitas, who treated us with sensible kindness, as much as possible.

For Dignitas ("Life with dignity, death with dignity"), the prerequisites for accompanied suicide are: old age (there have been quite a few folks in their nineties, who were not in pain but very, very tired), terminal illness (your inevitable death could still be ten years away—not acceptable in America; acceptable to the Swiss), or an "unendurable incapacitating disability" or "unbearable and uncontrollable pain." Dignitas,

founded in 1998 by Ludwig Minelli, a lawyer and the former
general secretary for the European Convention on Human
Rights, is occasionally accused of malfeasance (SWISS DROP
DIGNITAS PROBE OVER URNS IN LAKE, *The Seattle Times*, 2010;
CASHING IN ON DESPAIR? SUICIDE CLINIC DIGNITAS IS A PROFIT-
OBSESSED KILLING MACHINE, CLAIMS EX-WORKER, *Daily Mail*,
2009), but it has run pretty smoothly for these twenty-two
years. Occasionally, Dignitas has had to move facilities, from a
flat, where the neighbors objected, to Mr. Minelli's own home
in Maur, where his neighbors also objected, to another apartment in Zurich, quite close to a brothel, which objected for
obvious reasons, then to a bowling-ball factory, and now to
an industrial park in the suburbs of Zurich. Ludwig Minelli,
at eighty-eight, still seems to be running things. (Sandra Mar-
tino's name has popped up a couple of times; she is the chair-
woman in Germany, where Dignitas hopes to open an office
in the coming year, due to a federal-court ruling that the ban
on assisted suicide in Germany is unconstitutional.)

Pegasos is quite similar to Dignitas and, in fact, is related.
Dr. Erika Preisig worked for Dignitas from 2006 to 2008. She
went on in 2011 to co-found Lifecircle, an organization active
in supporting policy change around assisted suicide and pro-
viding counseling and support.

For more or less the same fee as Dignitas, with more or
less the same application process, although with the addition
of a second doctor interviewing you once in Switzerland,
Pegasos provides the same accompanied suicide that Dignitas does, but the barbiturate can be injected intravenously
(self-administered by turning a knob or pressing a button) or
drunk, and the death is recorded on video. Dr. Erika Preisig

and her brother, Ruedi Habegger, co-founded Lifecircle, but you can't find it anymore because in 2019, Dr. Preisig was fined twenty thousand dollars and sentenced to fifteen months in prison (suspended sentence) after a wrongful-death suit was successfully filed against her—for mishandling the barbiturate involved in the assisted suicide of a depressed sixty-year-old woman. The court found that this woman had the discernment to choose to end her life but that Dr. Preisig had mishandled (which I think meant *handled*) the sodium pentobarbital in assisting her. So, Dr. Preisig disappears and her brother opens Pegasos. Pegasos defines itself mostly as better than Dignitas: Less red tape! Urgent situations can be addressed in weeks, not months! English is the first language for the volunteers! You can bring your dog! No membership fees!

In English big-city newspapers (MY WIFE ENDED HER LIFE AT DIGNITAS, *The Guardian;* I'M ANGRY THAT DAD HAD TO DIE AT DIGNITAS SO FAR FROM HOME, *Daily Mail*), there are multiple articles every year about a husband or wife or children taking someone they love to Dignitas. It's usually a first-person account of the anxious plane ride (and in England, they usually keep it even more quiet than Brian and I will, because the police have been known to come to the house as soon as the grieving family returns and announce that charges are pending) and then the drive to the little blue apartment building, which some people call the Blue Oasis, in the industrial outskirts of the suburbs of Zurich. The articles sometimes end before the person drinks the anti-emetic, and sometimes an article goes on to describe the very end and the return home.

Dr. G. knocks on the door in the morning and begins by saying that it will be a short meeting. He asks Brian twice if he has changed his mind and Brian says no. He and Brian talk about their shared love of the Dalai Lama and they each get to tell their story about being a young man and meeting His Holiness. They are pleased with each other. I wipe my tears on my sleeve. Dr. G. asks Brian a few questions to make sure that Brian knows where he is (Zurich), why he's here (to have an accompanied suicide at Dignitas), and what will happen (have a chocolate, sign some papers, drink something so he won't vomit, and drink the drink, is what he says). Brian answers just right and it is one of those moments when the fact that he answers correctly makes me think, Are we doing this too soon? Should we come back in six months? After Dr. G.

leaves, and I cry some more and Brian is dry-eyed, I can see how far away he already is. His little boat is far offshore now.

We go out to dinner and eat not-bad Italian food and Brian orders with none of his brio. He doesn't look at the waiter. Brian knocks over my glass of wine and the waiter puts six cloth napkins on our little table and Brian sits calmly while the mopping up occurs and another waiter kneels beside me to clean up the broken glass. I'm sure we speak but only about the food and the weather. We walk down a few side streets, through the mist, and circle around to our hotel. As he has every night, Brian asks if we can go for a stroll and I say yes, because how can I say no. It is cold and dark and slippery and I imagine that Brian feels as alone as I do but I can tell he isn't as afraid.

Spring 2019, Stony Creek

Tell Me Why

Our normal life had begun to require a level of effort that I'd last had to make when I had an unhappy marriage, a full-time job, a teenager, a toddler, and a baby, with none of the joy. Having barely looked at another man or woman for fourteen years, I was now imagining myself having drinks on a rooftop lounge with pleasant but unlikely, even unpromising, companions. Brian and I were always stickily close; we liked to grocery shop together. We liked to go to the fish market and the bakery and the dry cleaner's together. He was as familiar with my shoes and shopping preferences as my sister was. I had even driven with him across New England to visit fancy fly-fishing stores. Now I exhaled when he went for a long walk and ruminated late at night that maybe I could get him a small apartment in New Haven (a studio seemed punitively small, so I thought a decent one-bedroom, in a walkable neighbor-hood), with some kind of helper, if needed.

How I could have contemplated "helper" and managed not to wonder *why* I was thinking that my sixty-five-year-old husband, who read Faulkner and worked out three times a week, would need a . . . helper, I couldn't—*absolutely could not*—say.

We would still do parental and grandparental things together, and I imagined that somehow the family would never have to know that I found it impossible to live with this man who I clearly adored. I didn't tell anyone in the world that I had these thoughts. I did tell close friends that he was driv-ing me crazy with his male mid-sixties/early retirement/loose ends. And it will pass, I said to myself, and look—he's mak-ing stained glass (I found the teacher, made the appointment for the lesson, and located the studio) and going to his book club (I scanned the planning emails when he felt overwhelmed and I ran to the library for the book) and he's pursuing the occasional zoning fights of our little town and studying the town's bylaws with great enthusiasm, so, really, what's wrong? I couldn't say, but I knew that this man was not the man I'd married, and the change had happened not over fifty years, which would have been very sad but not puzzling, but over three years. And since I still couldn't say anything about it to anyone, I certainly couldn't do anything about it.

I did the reading and I watched the videos and I pushed myself to see what I wasn't willing or able to see a year ago—Brian had had the signs of mild-to-moderate Alzheimer's since late 2016.

For the oldest son of a large Italian family, having a woman wait on him, or serve him, or assist him when assistance was desired (when it was not desired, there was no helping him at all) was pleasant and comforting; and, at least half the time, it was pleasant and comforting to me. I'd become a stepmother to a ten-year-old when I was twenty-one, and I liked that job more than I think most girls would have. I graduated from college, got and then quit the job of a lifetime at a theater in New York. ("My boyfriend thinks it's too hard to have a family and be in the theater," I said. Everyone was at least ten years older than I, and I think they felt the annoyed pity one does for lucky young people who don't know what they're throwing away. No one laughed or scolded me or took my car keys away. I moved back to Connecticut, moved in with my former professor and his son, and we became a family.) I took a job at a daycare center. I was home by three, so I could make cookies and play gin with my almost-stepson. I took him to doctors' appointments (where the nurse stared at us both in our nearly identical graphic T-shirts, shaggy hair, and drooping bell-bottoms and then shrugged), and I took a strong stand against his parents clothing him in earth-tone plaids, which made him look like a cholera victim. I shopped with him, played Othello and backgammon, tucked him in (when he wanted to be tucked in), cooked what he wanted to eat, insisted he write thank-you notes, and defended him against all comers. I was as good a parent as I knew how to be, because there was something about the job that mattered to me (well, not "something": my own mother, who was a loving presence and a terrible cook but never protected me from anything or anyone, handicapped as she was by besetting anxiety). I have liked caring and doing and protecting since my first round as a mother and got better at it with two more children, and by the time I got to Brian's early Alzheimer's—even though neither of us knew what it was—the steady ratcheting up of tactful assistance, comforting, protecting, and general back-leading was imperceptible to me.

But my dapper husband (I used to describe his professional wardrobe, admiringly, as gay Mafia hit man) refused to wear anything but a T-shirt and baggy jeans, and he took early retirement from a job that I knew he could do in his sleep.

Early Retirement

Brian got his last job four years ago, as a university architect, by being Brian, as far as I can tell. He described a
series of interviews, all kinds of questions about architecture,
interior design, and collaborative work. He said he told the
committee he was a team player (very true) and adaptable (not
very true). He came home feeling that he'd nailed it, heard
from someone on the interview committee that he had, and
was hired twenty-four hours after the interview. Neither of us
could tell, after a few months, exactly what the problems were.
I wondered why he seemed to have such poor communication
with the office manager and the administrative assistants and
why he got such a cool response, after a month, from his boss,
the woman who'd hired him with such enthusiasm.

He was disappointed and puzzled most days. He didn't
understand why so many things were going wrong. He en-

joyed lunch in the dining hall and it sounded as if he spent a lot of time there, eating and being chummy with the dining hall manager. He told me about meetings with his boss, and I could hear that he had brought his great charm to bear in those meetings and had won reprieve after reprieve, but I couldn't figure out what he had done—or not done—that required reprieves.

After a while, I stopped pressing him for details. I encouraged him to be extra-polite to the unhelpful and impatient office staff. It didn't seem to help at all. By summer, he met regularly with his boss, to keep track of his projects, since he reported that she told him he's "too slow." His boss called him in to ask if he's on any medication that might affect his concentration. We were both concerned and we both concluded that maybe the medication he was taking for pain (prior to his first hip replacement) was making him appear fuzzy, maybe *making* him fuzzy. We decided he should tell her about the pain medication and about scheduling his hip replacement for October. He told her and then told me that it went well.

He had his hip replacement and took eight weeks for his recovery. He stopped talking about life at the office and he didn't seem very busy. The printer and the computers and the office protocol baffled him, and deadlines flew by. Before Christmas, his boss told him that his contract would not be renewed next April. She emphasized that he was not being fired, just not renewed. Brian understood, as I did, that he was being fired, nicely. He cleared out his office at the university and told everyone that he was taking early retirement. He told me that his boss was a bean counter.

Writing this, I'm amazed and disappointed in myself,

blind in the bright light waiting another year and a half before we finally schedule the first appointment with the neurologist.

The neurologist brings us into the office, asks us some questions about Brian and his memory problems, gives him the mini-mental status exam, and then asks him to draw a clock. The instructions are: *Please draw a clockface, placing all the numbers on it. Now set the time to 10 past 11.* (Some places offer a

Mini-Mental State Examination (MMSE)

Patient's Name: _____   Date: _____

Instructions: Ask the questions in the order listed. Score one point for each correct response within each question or activity.

Maximum Score	Patient's Score	Questions
5		"What is the year? Season? Date? Day of the week? Month?"
5		"Where are we now: State? County? Town/city? Hospital? Floor?"
3		The examiner names three unrelated objects clearly and slowly, then asks the patient to name all three of them. The patient's response is used for scoring. The examiner repeats them until patient learns all of them, if possible. Number of trials: _____
5		"I would like you to count backward from 100 by sevens." (93, 86, 79, 72, 65, ...) Stop after five answers. Alternative: "Spell WORLD backwards." (D-L-R-O-W)
3		"Earlier I told you the names of three things. Can you tell me what those were?"
2		Show the patient two simple objects, such as a wristwatch and a pencil, and ask the patient to name them.
1		"Repeat the phrase: 'No ifs, ands, or buts.'"
3		"Take the paper in your right hand, fold it in half, and put it on the floor." (The examiner gives the patient a piece of blank paper.)
1		"Please read this and do what it says." (Written instruction is "Close your eyes.")
1		"Make up and write a sentence about anything." (This sentence must contain a noun and a verb.)
1		"Please copy this picture." (The examiner gives the patient a blank piece of paper and asks him/her to draw the symbol below. All 10 angles must be present and two must intersect.)
30		TOTAL

(Adapted from Rovner & Folstein, 1987)

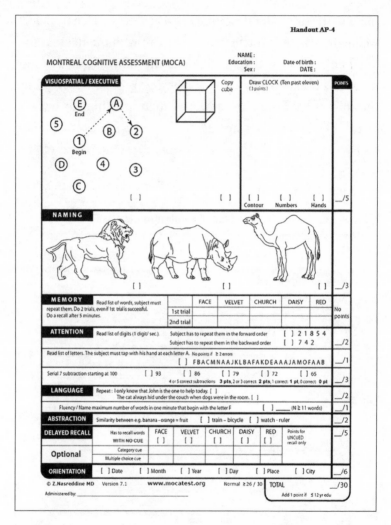

pre-drawn circle, but that's not as highly regarded an approach and it's not what the neurologist does.)

The maximum MMSE score is 30 points; 25 to 30 is a healthy person's score; 20 to 24 suggests mild dementia, 13 to 20

Interpretation of the MMSE

Method	Score	Interpretation
Single Cutoff	<24	Abnormal
Range	<21	Increased odds of dementia
	>25	Decreased odds of dementia
Education	21	Abnormal for 8th grade education
	<23	Abnormal for high school education
	<24	Abnormal for college education
Severity	24-30	No cognitive impairment
	18-23	Mild cognitive impairment
	0-17	Severe cognitive impairment

Sources:
- Crum RM, Anthony JC, Bassett SS, Folstein MF. Population-based norms for the mini-mental state examination by age and educational level. *JAMA*. 1993;269(18):2386-2391.
- Folstein MF, Folstein SE, McHugh PR. "Mini-mental state": a practical method for grading the cognitive state of patients for the clinician. *J Psychiatr Res*. 1975;12:189-198.
- Rovner BW, Folstein MF. Mini-mental state exam in clinical practice. *Hosp Pract*. 1987;22(1A):99, 103, 106, 110.
- Tombaugh TN, McIntyre NJ. The mini-mental state examination: a comprehensive review. *J Am Geriatr Soc*. 1992;40(9):922-935.

suggests moderate dementia, and less than 12 indicates severe dementia. On average, the MMSE score of a person with Alzheimer's declines about two to four points each year.

Brian gets a 23. Mild dementia.

The neurologist asks Brian some other questions and asks me some questions, too, which I am sorry to have to answer in front of him. (Even in that office, my wish to minimize and normalize is hard to resist. But yes, I say, he does forget things, he does repeat things from one conversation earlier in the hour and again forty-five minutes later. Yes, he has complained of some trouble with his balance.) He struggles with the mini-mental exam. He knows who the president is. He can't quite get the right month or season, and when he's asked to count backward by 7s, he says, I'm never gonna be able to do that. After the first appointment, the neurologist sends Brian off for a bunch of blood work and she says, He'll likely need an MRI. As we leave, the neurologist says, The MRI is necessary.

Ring the Bells

Meditation has been a great help to Brian, and therefore to me. My meditation is gardening, but Brian is old school and, after a long break from meditating, he's back and has been going to a Yale mindfulness program for the last few years. He's up and out the door at ten o'clock with the lunch I packed for him. He's back an hour later. He went to the wrong place. He went to Madison, where there's a meditation center he has visited a few times in the past, but the retreat today is in New Haven, at the usual Yale location. He's upset with himself and says that he's going to go upstairs and meditate. I tell him I'm sorry. I go outside and see that his car door is open. I close it and call out that I'm going to do a little gardening.

The next day, we go to a brunch nearby with old friends of Brian's from Yale. I tend to be the calendar-keeper (because I give a shit, is why) and I have had to rush us out of the house to get to the eleven o'clock brunch, twenty minutes away. We both look nice. We're looking forward to it—Brian to talk about Yale, past and present, and me because brunch is my favorite meal and the house is on the water. We drive up and there are no cars. The house is dark. Brian gets out and surveils. He even goes to the house next door—also dark. I check my phone. I have the right day of the week and the right time, but we are one *month* early.

I apologize several times, for rushing him as I often do, for messing up. He is as chill and relaxed and kind as a human can be. He laughs. He kisses me on the nose. He settles back in the passenger seat and says, "It's a beautiful day. We've got no plans. The world is our oyster." We decide that our preferred oyster is the diner up the road with the excellent sweet potato fries and Greek omelets, and that's where we go. The view is the parking lot, the coffee is weak but hot, and my husband squeezes in next to me in the booth. The world is utterly our oyster for hours. (*Ring the bells that still can ring,* I know.)

The next weekend are our back-to-back birthdays, June 18 and 19. I find that I can barely remember all the happy birthdays that I know we've had, because waves of grief knock them down. The waves of grief—which I had always thought of as representing a certain ebb and flow of feeling—turn out to be much more like actual waves, the big gray-green waves of the Atlantic Ocean. Thick, salty, consuming, and cunning, picking you up and throwing you down somewhere else, and you are not the better for it.

We are celebrating my birthday at a semi-swanky waterside

restaurant. I am teary from the time the waiter pours our water. I weep behind the big menu. I go into the ladies' room and cry some more. I come out and Brian is concerned but not upset or apologetic. I don't know why I was crying so hard, so unstoppably. A few months ago, he got me a very expensive and very odd present, a hooded marled sweatshirt with tulle trim for five hundred dollars. I still don't know what it was or why he bought it. I tend to wear black shirts and jeans. Sometimes navy shirts. Occasionally, white. In all of our years together, Brian—sensibly—never bought me anything with a ruffle, a flounce, or anything like tulle. I'm still surprised that I didn't look at that sweatshirt and think, I see that you have Alzheimer's. He had been giving me off-kilter cards, sequined hats on frolicking hamsters, for the last two years. His hand-writing (architect-neat) was now all swerving block print, and the sentiments seemed rote and flat in one (*you are so nice, sweet, funny, and beautiful*), and inside the other one, which I still cannot read without curling up, with grief and chagrin, it says: *I promise to be kinder to you.*

I suggest we go to the city for his sixty-sixth birthday and have a lovely overnight. I feel like an overnight is about what we can handle, and I hope that lovely is still possible. We haven't yet had our diagnostic neurology appointment, but I can feel something coming hard, a train rumbling through, startled birds flying off. Brian agrees and we go to the city. We relax in the pretty room, admire the courtyard, rest and shower, and Brian asks me if he needs to dress up. I shrug. Other women tell me that their husbands get to be this way as they get older, wanting to stay in their T-shirts and sweatpants, regardless of the occasion. I notice the mismatched straight couples: the woman's in cocktail dress and heels, and the guy has basically found a clean polo shirt and a belt. I am married to a man who owns two tuxes, four sets of studs, and plenty of cummerbunds, but we have had a lot of conversations about his dressing up or down the last couple of years. I say, as pleasantly as I can, Honey, wear what you want. You're a handsome man. He puts on his sports jacket with jeans and a white shirt. He puts on the glasses he recently bought (the last few years, his face had begun to look so vulnerable and unsure, I'd begged him to start wearing glasses again. He had missed them, he said, and then he started wearing them every day and we both felt that he was now properly armored). He looks, right then, exactly as he looked on our wedding day: handsome and expansive, at ease with himself and the world.

We have a quiet but lovely dinner at a very expensive Italian restaurant, and we have fun with every dish. *Trofie nero* and I forget the middle part; then, for dessert, Brian has *crema al cioccolato* and he makes me order the *mille-feuille*, which is also chocolate-intensive, and we take our time. We walk most of the way back to the hotel and then my shoes hurt and I say, Let's get a cab, and Brian says, Just a few more blocks, and I walk one more block and stop. He looks at me and says, Want a cab. I say, Yes, I do. He puts his arm up. We are both, I think, determined to have a nice time.

In the hotel, we begin to make love and Brian says, I'm sorry. Not gonna happen. I say, It's okay, and it is okay. That is the last time for that.

We kiss and sleep wrapped around each other.

• • •

Back at home the next day, we have one of our mutually mad-dening conversations: I tell Brian that I'm going to weed our picnic area (gravel with tons of weeds busting through). He says, as he has said repeatedly, that although he'd started add-ing the gravel six weeks ago on his own, he stopped because it aggravated his tennis elbow. I last heard about his tennis elbow five years ago. Also, he doesn't play tennis. The picnic area is big and bumpy with occasional mounds of gravel, as if giant moles are burrowing through it. Brian says we need a lot more gravel to make the area solid underfoot. He says we should hire someone to bring and spread the gravel. I agree and say that we can't afford to do that right now. (Also, I don't want another project to supervise, and since we can't afford to have it done professionally, however it's done, it will involve me working side by side with a helper. All I want to spend money on, all I really want to do, is buy shoes and clothes.) I tell him I'm going to weed and smooth out the gravel we do have. He tells me that we need more stone. I tell him that I agree but that we can't afford it. I tell him that I'll take care of it. He tells me we need more stone. I'm sure the look on my face is not a pleasant one. He says, Do you want me to do it? I say no, although I mean yes. I mean, Yes, if you could do it the way you would have a couple of years ago, measuring the number of cubic yards needed and discussing the size of the gravel until I want to scream—yes, that would be great. But not now. Now it would not be great and I would either be trying very hard to discreetly micromanage the entire time or else end up doing it myself, so, no. I go to my office to eat a scone and read a mystery and hope that I will clear my head and do some actual work.

I have studied up and watched dozens of English videos about this process (including the 2011 one featuring Sir Terry Pratchett, who died of Alzheimer's in 2015), and some of them are weirdly uplifting and some of them are unbearably sad, but not, for me, as sad as they will be. I also watched *Still Alice* a couple of times, on the sly. Julianne Moore, the actor, is beautiful and talented, and Alice, the character, is flirtatious and warmhearted and wise, and I enjoy the movie, sort of, until I find myself getting irritated with her winsomeness and unyielding charm, but at the end, when her former self tries to guide her current self, via prerecorded message, to suicide, I cannot watch. I walk in and out of the room a dozen times, each time willing Alice to bring the laptop with her to the dresser, to balance it properly, to not drop the pills but to manage to take them and achieve what her more-present self had hoped for. I watch this movie, in bursts, when Brian is working out or taking a walk. Everything else I watch is reality TV, which Brian despises, in which every character is a pretty shabby human being, or English comedies, specializing in the hilarities of class conflict, which he used to love.

Brian wakes up the next morning with stomach pains. He thinks he's constipated but he's also reporting bowel movements, so we're both stumped. His stomach is tender to the touch.

Me: Maybe you have appendicitis.

Him: I don't.

Me (thinking, *Why are you being stubborn and ridiculous?*): You could have—

Him: I had my appendix out years before I met you.

Me: Where's the scar?

Him: Have a look.

He stretches out like a white sea lion and rests his hand on the scar.

Off he goes to urgent care, five minutes from here. He insists on driving himself. I don't feel good about letting him go by himself (and this is the last time I will ever let him do that. All doctor's appointments are now joint business). He drives off. (For fourteen years, he beeped the horn every time he drove off, because he liked me to stand on the porch and wave goodbye, whenever possible. He has turned me into a wave-from-the-porch person, and I do it for everyone who pulls out of my driveway. Now people who don't do that for their guests seem to me to be lacking something, as I was.) I hear from him after about an hour. Someone (doctor, nurse, PA?) has told him a bunch of things at Stony Creek Urgent Care, which he mostly misreports (I think, but maybe not), scaring the shit out of me.

"An emergency MRI? What for?"

"I don't know."

I never get to speak to the doctor who sends him to New Haven for what I think are an ultrasound and bladder scan and blood tests. New Haven, which has been my home city for forty years now, feels to me like Rome at rush hour: confusing, dangerous, impossible to navigate solo. I have two appointments with patients, starting in a half hour. (When Brian retired three years ahead of schedule, I started doing psychotherapy again, in my little Stony Creek office. Smart to see that we were going to need the cash. Stupid not to have scheduled a neurology consult right then.) Between sessions, I talk to my dear friend and assistant, Jennifer, who's in New Haven, and when Jennifer asks if I'd like her to meet Brian in the ER (where he may or may not be having an emergency MRI, where he may or may not actually wind up), I cry and thank her. She meets him at the ER and keeps him company. She calls regularly and texts for the next three hours and is reassuring, every time. He doesn't need to see any specialists, there is no MRI, there was never an MRI, he's not being admitted to the hospital, and nothing is terrible. She says later, We had a great time, just goofing around. You know me and Brian, we joked about everything. He handled it all really well, she says, but sometimes he forgot what the doctor'd just said.

I'm pissed off. (I do not find myself yukking it up with Brian in ERs, or anywhere else, these days.) I want to point out that not understanding the doctor's directions is no one's idea of "handling it really well," but I'm crying too hard and I thank her, as I should.

Diverticulitis it is. Ten days of bland but not raw food, and some smooth peanut butter on white bread is okay but no peanuts or popcorn. Jennifer promised me that in Brian's diverticulitis info packet, there's a list of foods he should eat for the ten days of antibiotics and a few recipes for rice/dairy/chicken. There is no list. I am furious and frightened and turn to Dr. Google before I drive to the grocery store. It's a boring diet, especially for a man who loves chorizo, habanero sauce, Szechuan chili oil, and Popeyes chicken. I sympathize and keep offering rice and canned fruit and cheese and yogurt and baked chicken, and when he says, "How about chocolate?" for the third time, I just say no and then I go cry in the bathroom. He wouldn't have followed me out of the room fourteen years ago, and he's not going to start now.

The next day starts calmer and then not so much. Brian feels no worse and goes to the gym and buys a cable for the Garmin in his car. We've had a straightforward conversation about his need for a new GPS, and not his vintage version, which seems to be missing some important, smaller byways. He schleps all over eastern Connecticut, without me, and finally gets the cord he needs. He has been remarkably persistent and I admire him and I was scared witless when he'd been gone for five hours. I congratulate him and tell him all the bland goodies that await him. I wonder if I should hide his keys or if we will have to negotiate every drive for the foreseeable future. (We will.)

I sit down to work late in the day and Brian calls me: He has lost his keys (along with the groceries in the grocery cart) at our nearby Stop & Shop. I pick him up and we don't bother trying to retrieve our cart. Before dinner, the Stop & Shop manager calls Brian to say that the keys have been found. *But* Brian never checks his voicemail, so he doesn't know this. *But* I guess that the keys have been found and go there anyway and ask the manager, who says they do have the keys. *But* he can't give them back to me because I am not Brian. I go home to get Brian. *But* Brian is watching Rachel Maddow, and he doesn't want to go. I want to go. I want to get it done. I want just one fucking crisis to be resolved neatly and I would like it to be resolved today. Mutually annoyed, we go to the Stop & Shop and I walk in with him. Brian kids around with the manager and we walk out a few minutes later, Brian swinging his keys and whistling. Not relaxing.

Thursday, July 18, 2019, Stony Creek

MRI Day

The appointment for Brian's MRI is at eight forty-five and it's only fifteen minutes away. We both wake up at six-thirty. Brian lies in bed for a while, grumbling at his phone. He takes his morning meds and tells me he's contemplating a shower. I encourage the shower because he has a bad case of psoriasis on his scalp, and the only thing that keeps it from trailing into his eyebrows and erupting around his nose is the medicated shampoo he uses every day.

We have been talking about the psoriasis-shampoo-used-daily for about a year and a half. Looking back, it seems like a lot of fraught conversation to have about continuing to do something he's done almost every day for the fourteen years we've been together. He's a good-looking man. When we went to his Yale reunions, trim blond women, often married to other Old Blues, would toss their hair (even at our advanced age) and say, Oh, you're with Brian Ameche? *Thor?* You know, that was his nickname . . . when I knew him, they'd say.

My husband always smelled great and looked good and was vain about his good looks, his wolfish smile and his dark, thick hair. I didn't mind the vanity, which was not excessive and mostly shared only with me. About once a year he grabbed his stomach and said, If it was free, I'd get a tummy tuck. After he had his cataracts removed, he dragged me into the bathroom to look with him into the mirror. These bags, he said. You never told me. Six weeks later, he was getting an eye lift. When we'd go out to dinner and look out on a sea of men his age, even if we had been in a furious argument, he'd grin, tap me on the hand, and say, Howdya like me now? And I'd always laugh. I didn't understand why I was now having to say: Wash your hair, honey. Or, Honey, take a shower.

Now I understand. And now that I understand, I wish that it was middle-aged-man laziness, or retirement blues, or a man's response to being told what to do.

It's not. I've been reading and it's mild cognitive impairment, which is, as far as I can tell (our informative, post-MRI meeting with the neurologist will be next week), a wildly euphemistic name for the early stages of dementia, although all the medical websites quickly state that not every case of MCI turns into dementia. For some people, it's just a memory fog that never lifts but, in better news, it does not descend.

I turn my mirror to modest magnify (in L.A., a makeup artist told me that if you have a mirror that magnifies more than 3X, you'll never leave your house). I've put on mascara and moisturizer. I don't expect the technicians at the MRI center will like me more for putting on a little makeup. I am absolutely sure that they don't give a shit, but I was a bartender and I know no one likes a problem customer (loud, bedroom slippers, food on the sweater, smelling like piss). More effort than clean and pleasant is not required. Brian has always been our best shot at excellent customer care. Big, handsome man with a big laugh who says, Thank you for your help, or hard work, or advice—every time. We were once in a Starbucks with a barista-in-training our age, who was struggling. After the man delivered our coffees to us, Brian put five dollars in the tip jar and said quietly, "You're doing great. Don't let those punk kids throw you off." The man almost kissed him.

Brian is downstairs having his tea and I am still upstairs. I take a good look in the mirror. Under the tan, I'm gray. I could be any of my unlucky ancestors, facing a rifle, or a cattle car, or my burning village. I am wearing a white shirt and navy pants because it's summer in Connecticut, and I've brushed my hair in a reasonable manner (in what my daughters and I call an "elevated" ponytail, which is how I used to do my daughters' hair—with a Topsy Tail device—and how my oldest daughter does her daughters' now, and instead of satisfaction at the generational line of extra-nice ponytails, I just tear up. Elevated ponytail, are you kidding me, dead lady?). I've put on a pinkish lip gloss and I still look like a woman from a Munch painting. I see now how the clown-faced old ladies come to be. You look in the mirror, you do what you've always done, eyes, cheeks, lips, and still a dead woman looks back at you. What the hell. You darken your eyebrows, you redden your cheeks, you switch out from the neutral lipstick to a brighter one, and you just go out into the world, knowing that at least you don't look gray. I stay gray.

I'm walking around in my white shirt and underpants because I can't figure out if the navy pants are the right pants to wear. Maybe it's like trying to get upgraded in the airport. Maybe there will be a VIP waiting room at the MRI place. I know there won't be, and sure enough, we're seated with three people who look tired, ill, and furious. Brian comes back upstairs to see what's taking me so long. He says I look cute and pats my ass, and that drops me. I pretend to do something downstairs and cry for a minute on the landing.

We're both anxious, but our departure feels more normal than not. He walks out with his phone, wallet, protein bar, car keys, and sunglasses in his hand and I suggest he put them in his shoulder bag, so they don't get lost or left behind and so I don't end up carrying all of them for him. He gets his shoulder bag, which is a relief and also sad. Why shouldn't he just carry on in his usual blithe, chaotic way? Why should he have to now feel that I know better? I do know better, but I have known better for fourteen years and it's never made a difference.

At the MRI place, the techs are pleasant and bored. I've read up on things that make a head MRI easier. I've brought two Bill Evans CDs and headphones for my phone, in case they don't let us use the CDs. No headphones, the bored girl says. She adds, with more cheer, Your headphones would break. I ask if you can listen to music down at Yale when you have an MRI, and you can, and I curse myself for having been so selfish as to choose the nearby town, two exits away, with the easy parking instead of downtown New Haven, which is a pain in the ass but where Brian would have had music. He asks the women in scrubs what they advise about taking an Ativan.

"We don't offer sedations," one says.

"I know that," I say—I snarl. "I brought an Ativan. From home."

"Well," says the other, older woman primly. "He can take what was prescribed. We're not allowed to offer advice."

"I get it," I say. I am mentally writing my letter of complaint. No one gets an MRI of their head for casual purposes, and there is not a word or look of comfort or concern here.

On some website, it said a washcloth over the eyes helps the patient relax, and I have brought one and feel a little better about the music and myself. Brian takes the Ativan and lies down, washcloth over his eyes. I pull up a plastic chair and we put in our foam earplugs for what will be very loud, startling, occasionally percussive noise. I hold on to his leg. In between the noises, I shout things like "Hang in there, honey!" "You're doing great." I keep my hand on his leg the whole time. Sometimes, I touch his feet. He wiggles his toes back at me. This is my Brian: getting through the MRI steadily, wiggling his toes, occasionally keeping time to the noise, letting me know he's there.

This is exactly who I'm going to lose.

Every day is an up-and-down. (*Roller-coaster ride* makes it sound thrilling; it is not thrilling. The ups and the downs both hurt, it's a mistake to scream, and nothing moves quickly.)

While we wait to hear about the MRI results, we meet Ellen and her husband for dinner. I'm very close to my big sister, and the four of us always have a nice time. We're eating at their country club, which is never a comfortable fit for me but the food is good and we're happy to be with them. Brian has spent a lot of time in country clubs, due to his parents' brief, high-flying Main Line Philadelphia period, and he's designed one, so he's always comfortable and even enthusiastic about the setting. Everything is fine and normal. Brian orders two appetizers and an entrée and a dessert, and our brother-in-law, who is a man of moderate and healthful habits, shakes his head, one part disapproval to two parts affectionate admiration. A friend of theirs comes over and Brian is introduced to him (the guy already knows me). At the end of the meal, the man comes back again with his wife, for more chatting, and I notice, although I would rather not notice, that Brian introduces himself to the guy, as if for the first time. It's the only moment of forgetfulness.

On the way home, Brian and I have a very typical (as we used to be) chat about our brother-in-law's recent hip surgery. Having gone through two, Brian is a happy expert. We both think our brother-in-law should continue with physical therapy, as Brian did. Les has already expressed a lack of interest in that, and so has my sister. Brian and I have a very pleasant, self-congratulatory chat about how great it was that Brian continued with PT for a month longer than the minimum suggested and how well it's turned out for him. Aside from the fact that I'm driving, because I almost always drive now, his judgment seems fine. Brian now prefers to drive five and sometimes ten miles under the speed limit at all times (which is, perhaps, an example of very good judgment? If you know your decision-making skills are impaired, it certainly makes sense to drive more slowly and lessen the chances of a fatality). When I am driving, I don't have to notice his hesitation over which way to turn at an intersection we drive through weekly. The drive is like most of our drives: companionable and mildly entertaining. I see that falling asleep, cocooned and childlike, while my husband, a superior driver, takes us home has now been, in the words of Great Wayne, left behind in another country.

We get home. We go upstairs. Brian has always been the person who "buttons up" the house: doors locked, TV off, kitchen lights doused. Now, on the way up, he turns on all the exterior lights, which is a new thing in the last few months for him, but I don't argue, because (1) I try very hard not to argue anymore and (2) who knows? Maybe it's smart, in our little village, to turn on the outside lights. Maybe it keeps the kids from East Haven from breaking into our cars in the driveway—if we've left them unlocked. (These are the nicest juvie criminals ever. They don't even break a window. They open your unlocked car door and take whatever you've left in there. Then they close the door and drive away, in their own cars. I find it very hard to be angry or afraid about this. Also, I lock my car, every night. Brian doesn't, and sometimes now he leaves his car doors not only unlocked but ajar.)

In the bedroom, I recognize the hum of normalcy, and although I don't relax entirely, I do enjoy it. We brush our teeth. We smile at each other. He takes his vitamin B-12 supplement, which I hope is the answer to the question of what the hell is going on, but which I fear is not. (The descriptions of B-12 deficiency sound dire: suicidal wandering, yellow skin, deep dementia. That's not Brian.) We get out of our nice clothes. We throw the decorative pillows in a pile. I get into bed and Brian hands me the remote that adjusts our clock. He tells me to pick whatever show I want. The hum inside me stops. I hand the silver remote back to him and tell him what it is. He takes it silently. I get up and find the TV remote on the floor. Neither of us says anything. I have no idea if he thinks this is no big deal, which is how he's acting, or if this is the kind of psychic destruction he's trying to manage every day. We watch an episode of *Brooklyn Nine-Nine* and I say, I love Andre Braugher, and Brian says, Me, too.

Finally, we have our appointment, our second, with the neurologist. We get there in plenty of time. The secretary/receptionist nods at us from behind the glass. Two men in matching plaid shirts, one young, one old, are both slumped in the waiting room chairs, heads resting against the wall. The waiting room is so small, we all have to keep our feet tucked under us.

There are around six million people with Alzheimer's in the United States. This doesn't include the people with mild cognitive impairment who might or might not become more demented (statistically, 80 percent of people with MCI do go on to develop Alzheimer's within seven years, and although reevaluation every six months is recommended to people with

MCI, no website can tell you why frequent reevaluation is recommended, as there is no FDA-approved and successful treatment for MCI or for slowing the progression of MCI to Alzheimer's or, really, for Alzheimer's itself). The six million also doesn't include people with TBI (traumatic brain injury), which often leads to some form of dementia, or the people currently suffering from several different forms of dementia, which end just as badly as Alzheimer's but may progress differently. Almost two-thirds of these six million people are women. Almost two-thirds of the caregivers for those Alzheimer's patients are also women. More of the patients and more of the caregivers.

Women in their sixties are twice as likely to develop Alzheimer's as they are to develop breast cancer. There are a lot of theories about why more women than men get dementia, but only theories: Women live longer, so there are more ladies in their eighties still extant to get age-related dementia; the man who's living into his eighties didn't die of a heart attack in his sixties and seventies and is now a sturdier person compared to the women his age, who are often depressed and not regular exercisers. In 2005, there was a study of women's responses to estrogen and progesterone over four years. And in 2014, researchers conducted hormone-therapy trials on women in rural Utah, to see if women's brains, regardless of their health, wealth, and educational status, would respond to hormone therapy. It turns out, hormone therapy does a lot of good for a lot of women. And it may be that hormone therapy makes women less likely to develop Alzheimer's. "Lessening the likelihood of developing the disease" is a common phrase in the Alzheimer's universe, and it is used about getting enough sleep, eating blueberries, doing crossword puzzles, and a lot of things that are good for all of us, and no one, not one medical website, states that these good things actually prevent anyone—*anyone*—from getting Alzheimer's.

I don't have the scientific training to assess these theories. There are no comparable theories about why women make up two-thirds of the unpaid dementia caregivers, because no theories are needed. Scientists are not even interested enough to come up with theories about this, and I don't blame them. Who doesn't know? Sisters, daughters, wives. Of course they're going to take care of someone with dementia. Even the helpful websites for families and caregivers seem (gently) skewed toward female caregivers.

This below (from a dementia website) addresses how to get someone with memory issues to talk about it with his or her doctor.

HERE ARE SOME IDEAS TO CONSIDER WHEN TALKING TO SOMEONE ABOUT YOUR WORRIES.

- *Broach the topic gently. It may help to remind them that memory issues don't always point toward dementia.*
- *Be kind and supportive during the conversation. Listen to their reasons and any fears they raise.*
- *Let them know that you're worried about them. Give examples of issues: e.g., missing appointments, misplacing items, forgetting names.*
- *Break down the larger issue into smaller ones. Pick one to focus on: e.g., "I've noticed you've been forgetting names of friends. Maybe the primary physician will be able to help."*

- *Keep a diary of events as proof. This will help you show someone you're worried about that you have "evidence" for your worries. The diary will also support you both if you see a doctor, as they may want to see a record of issues.*
- *Turn the focus toward getting support for their friends and family: e.g., "If you visit the GP, we might be able to get extra help that would give me a break..."*

I don't disagree with any of this, above or below.

- *Let them know that you're worried about them. Give examples of issues: e.g. missing appointments, misplacing items, forgetting names.*
- *Break down the larger issue into smaller ones. Pick one to focus on: e.g., "I've noticed you've been forgetting names of friends. Maybe the primary physician will be able to help."*

I can see a wife approaching her more-than-forgetful husband from one angle (soft concern: "Darling, I thought you had book club tonight. Why didn't you go?") to another (provoking guilt: "I had a flat tire and I couldn't reach you. You didn't have your phone with you") and then another (prosecutorial: "I've asked you six times to take out the garbage and you haven't"). Since the problem keeps shifting, the approach should, too, but one is always a little behind. How do you assess the meaningful difference between *can't, won't,* and *don't remember being asked*? I write *I can see a wife* because I am that

wife. I spent three years trying to figure out who my husband
had become and how it was that whenever he was returned
to me, from time to beautiful, relieving time, neither one of us
could get him to stay.

- *Be kind and supportive during the conversation.*
  Listen to their reasons and any fears they raise.

I'm not sure how any husband or wife does it, responsively
and genuinely listening to the arguments and fears, a mix of
reasonable and not, and staying at all times, as instructed, gen-
tle, kind, and supportive. In the couple of years before Brian's
diagnosis, our fights changed, and one of the changes was that
he would complain not just about my being stubborn (yes), or
bossy (Jesus, yes), or a pain in the ass about precise language
(no lie), or fussy about clutter (suddenly), but for the first time
in all our years, he complained about my tone of voice: Do
not speak to me in that tone of voice, he'd say. I'm not a child.
I'm not your patient.

I don't doubt that I used a soothing, neutral, "therapeutic" voice, as therapy is usually performed on TV. I'd become
wary and worried about his mood swings, about the surprising
responses and misunderstood signals. I found myself saying,
often, "I don't understand what you're saying." Which might
have been a tactic once upon a time (I do feel it beats saying,
What the hell are you talking about?) but now that was exactly
what I meant. He would describe a problem or a situation at
the beginning of the sentence and wind up with a grand con-
clusion or crooked metaphor at the end. When I said that I
didn't understand, he'd repeat it. When I tried to interpret the

metaphor ("Maybe you mean . . ."), he looked disappointed
and frustrated and said, "We're not on the same page," which
was true and terrible. If I asked again, he sometimes said that
I was bullying him, which made me cry on the spot. I tried to
understand the new, stubborn resistance to things that he had
always not only enjoyed but pursued. Every Monday, he'd say
he was tired of going to the gym, or the book club, or stained-
glass lesson, and after the diagnosis, I just agreed, and he kept
up with the gym anyway (working out with his trainer, keeping
himself in shape because every Alzheimer's website says: *sleep,
exercise, blueberries*). He went every week to the stained-glass studio (a last joy, and after the summer, he knew it was), and I had
nothing to say about the book club. He was probably right
about my tone, but I couldn't find a better one.

> • *Keep a diary of events as proof. This will help you
> show someone you're worried about that you have
> "evidence" for your worries. The diary will also sup-
> port you both if you see a doctor, as they may want
> to see a record of issues.*

I don't know how any spouse or child produces the "diary
of events as proof" one afternoon and does not find themselves in a very difficult situation. (I can hear myself, if I was
the patient: "You wrote all this shit down? Why didn't you
just tell me?") Further on, the website suggests that if your
spouse is not having it, you call the doctor yourself and share
your concerns, without violating HIPAA (and the doctor is not
likely to share your partner's medical information with you in
that call, but you don't need them to). Then, when you have

set up the doctor's appointment, using some not-quite-bogus concern—fatigue, hearing loss, prediabetes, arthritis flare-up—and gotten your spouse to agree, you lug in the diary and hope to God your doctor is good at this. If they are, most likely your doctor will send you and your spouse to a neurologist for some tests, something like the clock-drawing or the mini-mental status exam.

The Clock-Drawing Test and the
Mini-Mental Status Exam

There are a lot of things a person with MCI could get wrong on these. At the worst end of the spectrum, they can't draw a clock at all, or the person draws a clock that doesn't look like a clock, in that it is not a circle or rectangle with numbers going around it. The most common results for those with dementia are: wrong time, no hands, missing numbers, the same number more than once, and a refusal to draw the clock. There are at least fifteen different scoring systems for the clock-drawing test. Most can be given and scored by an intelligent layperson, and most research shows that the simplest scoring system is as informative as the most complicated. If you can't ace the clock-drawing test, you probably have some kind of cognitive dysfunction. If you can do well on it, whatever is wrong with you is probably not dementia.

In our second appointment, the neurologist gets down

to it. (The neurologist says that Brian's MRI has now been read by some brilliant colleague, but the neurologist still has a few questions.) Brian has a high IQ and a high EQ—he's emotionally aware, the neurologist says. The people at the NeuroAging Institute are going to be delighted to have him in their studies: high IQ and early-onset Alzheimer's is apparently as appealing as tall and blond is in America. Then we hear a long digression about why and how the NeuroAging Institute people are really Yale people but no longer part of Yale and, if they do find a cure for Alzheimer's—I would roll my eyes but I am crying like my face is broken—Brian, as a participant in a clinical study, would be right at the head of the queue. Brian and I both get the basics: Brian probably (in a tone that says "definitely") has a dementing disease. It's probably Alzheimer's. Very, very likely. I ask if it seems to be vascular, the result of a big stroke neither of us ever noticed, from which he is still recovering. She says, No, but there have been some ministrokes in the cerebellum. I plan to look up *cerebellum* and what it does as soon as I get home. It deals with motor activity, balance, and . . . driving.

I say, So this thing at NeuroAging is for a second opinion, that maybe it's not Alzheimer's? I can see the neurologist is sorry to have to say, Not really, it would be for an evaluation, to provide more information. It's clear this doesn't mean *different* information or *contradictory* information, and I appreciate—for a minute—that it takes real discipline not to soften or deflect from the fact that Brian has Alzheimer's.

She asks if Brian is incontinent and she asks him to walk

around. I'm sure this is to confirm something about his balance, but I don't ask what. (In the next three months, his balance will become a problem, but not yet.) She tells him to
continue taking vitamin B-12 forever, although that's unlikely
to be the basic problem. But still. Maybe, the B-12 supplement
will help. ("It can't hurt," I hear my father yelling from the
Jewish Joke Playbook.)

Does it seem to be frontal-lobe, I ask (frontal-lobe dementia moves even more quickly than Alzheimer's, is what I read).
The neurologist says no.

The neurologist shows us the MRI, running a finger over
the white splotches on the round gray shape of Brian's brain.
I hear that line of Diane Ackerman's: . . . *the brain, that shiny
mound of being, that mouse-gray parliament of cells . . . that wrinkled
wardrobe of selves stuffed into the skull like too many clothes into a gym
bag.*

Brian's brain is in the slow process of unwrinkling, the
gym bag emptying out. I see the white spaces where the brain
no longer is, and so does he.

The neurologist runs a finger very gently over the amygdala on the MRI image. Probably something here, she says.

His brain is smaller than it should be at sixty-six—the
amygdala, in particular—and the ventricles are bigger. The
amygdala, this inch-long almond, deep in the temporal lobes,
above the brain stem, catches my eye and takes me right back
to high school biology. I say, Amygdala—that's feelings and
memories and learning? The neurologist nods, just once. I say
that on the websites, and I mention Mayo Clinic (she nods several times approvingly), they describe the Alzheimer's trajec-
tory as three to four to twenty years. The neurologist disagrees.

"Eight to ten to maybe—maybe—twelve. But remember, he's had these symptoms for at least two, I'd say three years." Every Alzheimer's website now states that people have Alzheimer's for ten, sometimes twenty years before the early symptoms emerge. The neurologist makes clear that those eight to ten to twelve years for Brian would be the end of life, the end of his body's life.

I have now watched enough Alzheimer's diary videos (*Who records this grief and posts it on YouTube? Who does this?* I think, even though I am as grateful as I am horrified) that it's very clear that the end of the body will be long after the end of the self. I see that in my notebook I wrote, on four different pages, *Possibly Alzheimer's,* which is surprising because I already have no doubts at all.

By moving to the practical, the neurologist signals that we are coming to the end of the appointment. (Maybe she can't take it anymore, which I understand. Brian doesn't move an inch, but the affect he usually shows the world is unchanged: affable and easy. I am in a wet fury that this is all the help we will get.) She says that Brian probably should not be driving, even with the GPS, not because he'll get lost (because of our directional impairment, we barely get where we wish to go, even with the GPS. In the good old days, we once spent an hour in a hotel parking lot, unable to find the exit) but because . . . Brian jumps in: I might be in an accident. You might kill someone, the neurologist says. We are both silent. I figure we will get Lyft on his phone over the weekend. (We do. He can't figure out how to use it.)

She tells me to go through his wallet and take out most things, all but one credit card, and put in a card with my info

on it. She seems to be describing a person who can no longer manage an independent life and I think this cannot be so,
because I saw him just that morning, making his oatmeal, with
lots of maple syrup and a handful of almonds, and a cup of
black tea, spreading *The New York Times* out before him, with
the air of a man getting down to work.

The neurologist asks Brian if he's the kind of person who
gives his info to strangers. He says no, with a laugh, and he
adds that he is a very Italian person and his innate paranoia
and xenophobia will work to his advantage here. He says these
words—*paranoia* and *xenophobia*—and I think, See?! See, Doc?

No matter how I fight this, at every sentence, I also see
that Brian's world is about to get very small. One of his great
pleasures is overdoing it with the groceries, involving several
stops at little markets, cheese shops, the East Haven lady
who makes her own Thai BBQ sauce and fries up a bag of
plantains for him while he waits. At our old house, we had a
refrigerator just for condiments. Even now, my older daughter
always says, How can you be only two people and never have
an empty fridge? That's Brian, I say, buyer of burrata, sop-
pressata, Meyer lemons, white peaches, Benton's ham.

On the way home from the neurologist, who has reminded
us to call NeuroAging and to come see her again sometime
but no hurry, I offer to drive to Liuzzi's (a great Italian deli)
and he says no. I am as disappointed and stunned as if I'd
offered him a blow job on a Sunday night and he'd said he'd
rather watch some Scottish mystery.

We get home and we cry for an hour, in each other's arms.
We agree not to do much talking for twenty-four hours. We
go out for sushi at our favorite restaurant and are waited on

by our favorite waiter, a Japanese man with a strong Japanese accent, whose conversational patter is like that of a Midwestern waitress: "How you folks doin'? Hot enough for you? C'mon, let's get you seated right here. Comfy? Has the summer been good?"

We love Hari, and we have a great, surreal couple of hours.

The weekend seems vast. I don't plan to work. We cancel a visit with friends. It's just us and I've let my grown children know that "we're processing," which they understand correctly to mean: Give us a few days. (Later, they will each reveal to me the changes that they had noticed in Brian—the slips in memory, the repetitions—and their loving, generous dismissal of those changes.) We go out to buy stationery—*Goodbye, I love you* stationery, so that he can write little notes to my kids and our grandchildren for after he's gone, because he has already made up his mind to end his life. (I'd rather die on my feet than live on my knees, he says and will say again. He has already told me to figure out how.) He'll also write cards to his mother and four siblings, but by the time he does that, I have to prod him.

I point out the elegant box of notecards with dragonflies. He points out a box with a porch overlooking a lake and four dogs sitting cutely on the Adirondack chairs. I point out that we don't have dogs. (We don't want dogs. I am already hearing people talk about dogs. Even my beloved Wayne suggests that maybe we'd want a dog now. I think I yelled that I did not want a fucking dog, that I have a husband with Alzheimer's,

three children, and four granddaughters, and I didn't need
another goddamn mammal to look after. I think that's what I
said. Wayne nodded. "No dog, then.")

In the Hallmark card section, Brian and I fall into each
other's arms and cry very hard for a couple of minutes. No
one gives us a second glance. I point out a box of cards with
the pen-and-ink drawing of a lighthouse. Brian nods and
shows me the box next to it, with Snoopy on top of his red
doghouse, typing furiously on a glittering typewriter. These,
he says; these'll make 'em smile. Then we cry again, as if we
are in our own bedroom, and again there is not even a concerned or disapproving glance. I tell him that he is amazing
and my hero. On line, I see a bunch of profane potholders.
I show him the one that says, *Fuck this shit,* and he laughs out
loud.

We get mango smoothies next door, from a sulky girl who
has clearly never ever made one, and we both feel, in this
moment, that this shabby little plaza, with the Hallmark store
right next to the empty Edible Arrangements store, is our new
favorite place.

Our whole weekend is crying and talking and binge-watching
TV at night. We're not people with conventional moral com-
passes, but we don't let ourselves binge-watch during the day.
We do things: We weed, we buy cute dresses at the outlets for
all four granddaughters, we go to a movie in the late afternoon, and usually, right after weeping in each other's arms,
we fall into deep naps, as if clubbed. We wake up and discuss
the garden, or the news, or the summer's end—we talk about

Stony Creek Market's Pizza Nights coming to an end at Labor Day and not about Brian's decline. We talk about the grandchildren, who use him and abuse him as loved granddaughters do, braiding his hair, flinging themselves on his soft stomach, pretending to be tiny football players, trying to get past him with the swim move (a pass-rushing technique used by defensive linemen, is what I understand), with which the three oldest are quite familiar. Before we fall asleep, Brian muses aloud about his wish to control his death and how I will arrange that for him. He'd made up his mind after forty-eight hours and never wavered. We cried and I agreed and he said to me, You go research it. You're so good at that stuff—which meant that while I was looking up Exit International and the Hemlock Society and websites that would sell you both the plastic turkey bag and the helium machine for your own painless (they kept saying) DIY suffocation, I was also researching how to get sodium pentobarbital—fifteen or twenty grams, which is a ton—on the dark web. I was discovering the limits of my friends with medical degrees and the possibilities of carbon monoxide poisoning, which you can do in your car in your garage, but it's become more iffy since 1975, when the car industry adjusted the CO emissions and then applied catalytic converters. Also, we don't have a garage.

As we are spreading out all these possibilities between us, we occasionally bump into an offer or a roadblock from a close friend. A dear friend offers her garage and I hug her and we cry, but she calls me a day later and says her spouse says no, too risky to help us. Brian's dearest oldest friend, his fishing buddy since 1979, says to Brian, "If you think you don't need to go right now, and you want to wait awhile, I can just shoot you myself, in a year or two, in a field." Brian hugs him. One of his brothers makes the same offer, and when Brian declines and points out that his brother could go to jail, his brother shrugs. "I'd be fine in jail. I don't go out much anyway." I have never liked the man more.

I look up *how it feels to drown* (that's all you have to type in; lots of people have first-person accounts about near-drowning, and they seem divided between peaceful brain fog as the white light shines brighter and clawing one's terrified way through terrible suffocation) and how *to* drown. Someone had told me about a friend of his in her late seventies with inoperable cancer, who filled her pockets with rocks and walked into the Connecticut River, which was, my friend said, practically in their backyard. I thought about it. Maybe we would need a small boat, since no river ran through our yard. Maybe we would need a small boat? I started looking for one on Craigslist one evening. For the next few nights, I woke up to visions of Brian and me, bundled in winter jackets, late at night, dragging the rowboat to our neighbor's dock and launching it. Would I be in it with him or just wave to him from shore? If I wasn't with him, how would he remember to take a few Percocet from his pocket so he wouldn't feel pain but would still be alert enough to tip himself out of the boat? It kept me awake nights and ruined my mornings, but I thought, Maybe he'll see it differently? I thought, This is what crazy looks like, and I thought, Nevertheless. I mention that drowning is a way some people end their lives. Brian looks at me, hard. "Are you kidding me? It's cold. No."

I say that I think that whatever method he chooses, I would like to be with him. "If that's okay," I say, as if this is only a second date and I don't want to be one of those clingy women who are always pushing to find out the status of the relationship. (This—dating—is not something I actually know about. I have barely been on a date, as such, since I was nineteen. Later, Great Wayne points out that widowhood might finally be my opportunity to be single. "Your first opportunity as an adult," he says, to underline that it's been forty-seven years with only minute interruptions.)

"Here's my first choice," Brian says. "We go through this process and whenever it is that we reach the point that it seems like I'm really going downhill, you tell me and then we lie down together, maybe in my office, not in our bedroom—well, maybe in our bedroom, we'll see—and you give me whatever will kill me. I trust your judgment."

"I can't do that, darling. It'll be murder. I can't give you something that will kill you. We read about that all the time. These people can be prosecuted," I say, although I don't really think that a white woman my age will be sent to do hard time for assisting her husband in ending his life, in Connecticut, the Land of Steady Habits, as Brian often calls it.

"I could go to jail. To jail."

Brian thinks this over and seems to drift away and then he comes back, with enthusiasm.

"You'd do great in jail. You're so resourceful; you're a leader. You'd be great."

I tell him that I won't do that and that whatever we do, it has to be his hand that guides the end. He falls asleep. In the depth of Google wormholes for end of life, for suicide, for assisted suicide, for euthanasia, for terminal illness, and for making end-of-life choices, in August I finally find Dignitas, a

Swiss organization to which even a foreigner can apply for an accompanied suicide, if you meet their criteria: be of sound mind, have medical records supporting this, have ten thousand dollars to commit, and be sufficiently mobile to get to the outskirts of Zurich. I am already imagining how we can get to Zurich, and I cannot really imagine how we (mostly me, with no medical training and limited hand-eye coordination) will do this at home if Dignitas doesn't work out. (They emphasize the words *application* and *provisional*, many times.)

Right to Die

R ight to die in America is about as meaningful as the right to eat or the right to decent housing; you've got the right, but it doesn't mean you're going to get the goods. After Brian told me his decision, I'd called End of Life Choices New York, where my daughter knew a woman who knew a woman. Their mission is "to expand choice at the end of life, respecting every individual's wishes, and striving for the best possible quality of life and a peaceful death." On their website, it says that they also strive to educate people about end-of-life choices. They have been able to accomplish making it legal in New York to at least tell dying people about palliative and hospice care, and they managed to get a law passed in 2011 that asserts that these people have the right to know about the care available to them. They educate, they advocate, they pursue, and, perhaps most effectively, they counsel.

I called the excellent and *haimish* clinical director, Dr. Judith Schwartz, to talk about the organization, but first she had to counsel me, since I burst into tears as soon as she answered the phone. She advised me right away about what she—and the organization—could and couldn't do. They do policy, they fight to expand the right-to-die laws so that you do not have to be in the final stages of a terminal illness to receive aid and medical assistance, and they attempt to ensure that, at the very least, your spouse or friend will not face prosecution if they do assist you in ending your life. ("Unsupervised two-year probation" is often what the widow who holds the gun or pours the poison winds up with, but that's after an arrest, legal wrangling, and headlines in your local newspaper.)

Dr. Schwartz says, "When any kind of right-to-die legislation is proposed—the opposition shows up with ten million dollars as soon as it's about your right to choose."

End of Life Choices New York supports VSED—voluntary suspension of eating and drinking—as the only effective, legal, and certain end to life that even a very physically limited person can choose. It sounds to me like it takes enormous discipline and fortitude for everyone. I had a friend, years ago, who sat by the bedside of a dear friend, holding her hand every day for weeks. She said it was peaceful at first and then excruciating and then over. It seemed to me that my friend was a better, and also just different, person afterward.

"It's not easy," Dr. Schwartz says.

I say, "It takes a couple of weeks, I know."

There's a pause.

"How big's your husband?" she asks, and I can tell her

exactly because, thanks to an eating-disordered adolescence of football *and* wrestling, Brian announces every change in his weight like a supermodel. "He's six foot one, two fifteen." (When he got the diagnosis, he dropped ten pounds in a minute. When he finished the application to Dignitas, he gained it all back and ate like a man on a mission and was, as always, happy to share, happy to order more, happy to meet the chef.)

And Judith Schwartz says, "Oh. Could be three weeks, even a week more." She says kindly, "It is not an easy process, often."

From which I take that *often* means *ever*, just as *rarely*, in all of my conversations now, means *fucking never*. She lets me know, because I ask twice, that her organization does nothing at all in the hands-on department.

"Oh, no," she says immediately but still warmly. I love Judith Schwartz as I now love everyone I speak to who is not cruel, horrified, or utterly useless in this process.

I ask what she has heard about Dignitas.

"Oh, yeah, they are the real deal," she says, and I am reassured once more that they are not scam artists (although in May 2018, BBC News reported that an ex-employee accused Mr. Minelli, the director, of receiving bequests from rich and more or less satisfied and grateful families of the dead. Who can blame them? To have your beloved relative find a way to painlessly end a life of suffering or of painful diminishment or of just plain exhaustion at one hundred four, like David Goodall, the ecologist and botanist, who said, "My abilities have been in decline over the past year or two, my eyesight over the past six years. I no longer want life to continue. I'm happy to have the chance . . . to end it").

I have now read everything, pro and con, about Dignitas

and seen most of the documentaries. Dignitas seems to do what it says it does: You fill out the forms, write the essays (a biography and a few paragraphs on why you wish to have "an accompanied suicide"), and send them—eventually—ten thousand dollars (more for the cremation and the mailing of the ashes in a plain urn if that's what you want, is what I recall) and a pile of documents. You show up in Zurich and they interview you, twice (it used to be only once, but someone complained that more assessment was required, and I assume that that someone was connected to the Swiss government), and you bring all sorts of identification, so it's not a pain in the ass for the Swiss police to identify the body (which apparently had sometimes required a couple of calls to grieving Americans, once they got back home).

"They're Swiss," Judith Schwartz says, laughing a little. "Here's what they're looking for: discernment. Discernment." She says the word emphatically, as does the woman—friend of a friend—who brought her father to Dignitas last year and has become my coach for the final-days part of the process—as if it's a word with special meaning, which it may be to the Swiss people, or to Dignitas. "Dis-cern-ment," she says. "You really have to be cognitively with it. That's what they're looking for and checking for. They absolutely will not accept anyone who cannot clearly make this choice, with full comprehension and understanding, from beginning to end."

They now require the dental records of the person coming to Zurich, and I have to get them. I mention this to Dr. Schwartz, with an air of can-you-believe-it?

"Just do what they tell you," Judith Schwartz says.

And I do.

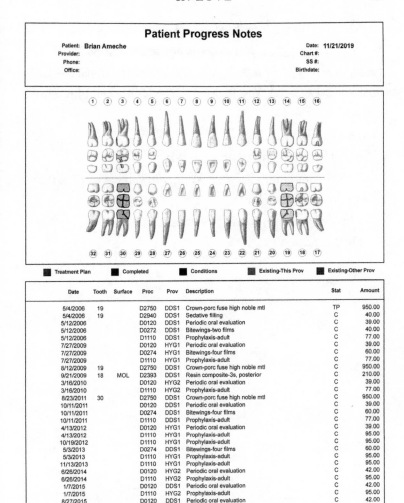

Patient Progress Notes

Patient:	**Brian Ameche**		Date:	**11/21/2019**
Provider:			Chart #:	
Phone:			SS #:	
Office:			Birthdate:	

Legend: ■ Treatment Plan ■ Completed ■ Conditions ■ Existing-This Prov ■ Existing-Other Prov

Date	Tooth	Surface	Proc	Prov	Description	Stat	Amount
5/4/2006	19		D2750	DDS1	Crown-porc fuse high noble mtl	TP	950.00
5/4/2006	19		D2940	DDS1	Sedative filling	C	40.00
5/12/2006			D0120	DDS1	Periodic oral evaluation	C	39.00
5/12/2006			D0272	DDS1	Bitewings-two films	C	40.00
5/12/2006			D1110	DDS1	Prophylaxis-adult	C	77.00
7/27/2009			D0120	HYG1	Periodic oral evaluation	C	39.00
7/27/2009			D0274	HYG1	Bitewings-four films	C	60.00
7/27/2009			D1110	HYG1	Prophylaxis-adult	C	77.00
8/12/2009	19		D2750	DDS1	Crown-porc fuse high noble mtl	C	950.00
9/21/2009	18	MOL	D2393	DDS1	Resin composite-3s, posterior	C	210.00
3/16/2010			D0120	HYG2	Periodic oral evaluation	C	39.00
3/16/2010			D1110	HYG2	Prophylaxis-adult	C	77.00
8/23/2011	30		D2750	DDS1	Crown-porc fuse high noble mtl	C	950.00
10/11/2011			D0120	DDS1	Periodic oral evaluation	C	39.00
10/11/2011			D0274	DDS1	Bitewings-four films	C	60.00
10/11/2011			D1110	DDS1	Prophylaxis-adult	C	77.00
4/13/2012			D0120	HYG1	Periodic oral evaluation	C	39.00
4/13/2012			D1110	HYG1	Prophylaxis-adult	C	95.00
10/19/2012			D1110	HYG1	Prophylaxis-adult	C	95.00
5/3/2013			D0274	DDS1	Bitewings-four films	C	60.00
5/3/2013			D1110	HYG1	Prophylaxis-adult	C	95.00
11/13/2013			D1110	HYG1	Prophylaxis-adult	C	95.00
6/26/2014			D0120	HYG2	Periodic oral evaluation	C	42.00
6/26/2014			D1110	HYG2	Prophylaxis-adult	C	95.00
1/7/2015			D0120	DDS1	Periodic oral evaluation	C	42.00
1/7/2015			D1110	HYG2	Prophylaxis-adult	C	95.00
8/27/2015			D0120	DDS1	Periodic oral evaluation	C	42.00
8/27/2015			D1110	HYG2	Prophylaxis-adult	C	95.00
3/1/2016			D0120	DDS1	Periodic oral evaluation	C	42.00

Page: 1 of 2

. . .

Dental Office Manager (who may be the dentist's wife): Is Brian changing dentists? Is he unhappy with Dr. L.? He's been a patient of ours for so long that . . .

Me (thinking, *My husband would never ever give up a dentist who likes football, saw Brian play magnificently in the Yale Bowl, and is a paisan, to boot. But we have to go to Zurich with his dental records so Brian can die in peace*): Yes, he loves Dr. L. I just need his dental records.

DOM: Yes, but . . .

Me: I just need his dental records.

DOM (thinking, *Fuck you*): Well, you'll have to pick them up in person. Before lunch.

Me: See you tomorrow morning.

DOM: *Click.*

September 2019, New Haven

We pin our hopes on Dignitas because the right-to-die laws in America are not going to help us. Dignitas leads me to a meeting with Brian's psychiatrist, because Heidi of Dignitas has told me that since Brian is in therapy, they need a report on his mental health from his psychiatrist. I'm sure that Brian's psychiatrist already knows the results of Brian's MRI test, because I can use the World Wide Web and I have learned that Brian's neurologist and his psychiatrist are not only the same age, practicing in the same city, but I already know they refer patients to each other and I see they went to the same medical school. I picture them having dinner together a couple of times a year. I picture the neurologist summing Brian up for the psychiatrist, over a couple of glasses of pinot grigio: Not good. His brain has shrunk. Lots of white stuff. A 23 on his mini-mental—23. Yale graduate. They both shake their heads.

It will turn out that these two doctors are for me the villains of this story. When I write fiction, there is almost always no villain at all. There are occasionally cruel fathers, often redeemed in the end by one great, embarrassing love affair or revealed to have a streak, however narrow, of compassion or decency. There are plenty of faithless wives in my fiction, but if you read carefully they are rarely villains, being married as they are to deeply disappointing men. Sometimes these women seem a little chilly, clipped in their remarks and short on hugs, but I like them.

A colleague described Brian's psychiatrist as above-average intelligence, below-average social skills. For better or worse, I know a lot of shrinky people, of all valences: social worker, psychologist, psychiatrist. Brian has told me he thinks his psychiatrist is smart and low-key and that she likes him. I don't think Brian has ever had a therapist who did not genuinely like him.

Years ago, he'd come home from sessions with his then-therapist, a revered New Haven psychoanalyst, and when I'd ask how it went—and, yes, I am familiar with and supportive of the idea that his therapy is not my business—Brian might say, We talked a lot about Yale's football program this season. We talked about Carm Cozza (Brian's football coach at Yale). We talked about the early days of lacrosse at Yale (they recruited some football players, stuck a lacrosse stick in Brian's hands, and sent him across the field to frighten people). I know that they also talked about Brian's struggles with his father, and our new marriage, and the challenges of being an architect in architect-filled New Haven, but he did report that they spent quite a bit of time happily shooting the shit. The new psychiatrist, however, seems to be all down to business with the inner life, and I am glad of it.

The new doctor will be important to us, to support Brian's claim of being "of sound mind." I tell Brian my thoughts and he hands me his phone. Let's get a meeting, he says. I have a text exchange on my phone with the psychiatrist. I ask if she has noticed some issues with Brian's cognitive function and she says yes.

I suggest we have a joint meeting (the three of us). The psychiatrist types back that Brian needs to be the one to arrange this meeting. I think, Yeah, yeah, I know. I was a clinical social worker for twenty-five years, I'm aware. I text something like: *Also, perhaps you recall referring Brian to a neurologist a while ago, for cognitive assessment, which was followed by an MRI, all of which—any of which—might lead you to think that Brian arranging an appointment on his own (remembering, scheduling, and reporting) might be difficult?* (I don't think I'm managing my text tone very well, but she doesn't know me and she may think that I'm just . . . brusque.)

Psychiatrist: *Yes, I recall.*

I calm down. I ask if we can meet in a few weeks.

Psychiatrist: *If Brian requests the meeting, yes, of course.*

Brian looks over my shoulder. Text her back as me, he says, and request a meeting. I do.

After the MRI report, the psychiatrist moves to the top of our list. We'll meet to discuss the results of the mini-mental status exam, and by the time we do meet with the psychiatrist, the neurologist's report has become an obstacle to Dignitas, and I am on the hunt for a psychiatrist or a neurologist to rebut it. It erroneously describes Brian as depressed, which, if true, would guarantee a *no* from Dignitas—making the psychiatrist's support a necessity.

At what will be our only meeting, the psychiatrist cannot conceal her distress when we tell her that having understood the diagnosis and the MRI, Brian and I are looking at Dignitas. As often happens with relatives and healthcare providers, a vacation, a final trip to Ravenna or Telluride or perhaps marlin-fishing in the Keys, is suggested. I know that, even if they have not watched the ten thousand YouTube videos on Alzheimer's and its progression, medical professionals do know that no one can predict how quickly or slowly Brian's particular case will progress. Whether you are medical personnel, clergy, worried child, or hopeful spouse, you do know, even if you never say so, that this disease progresses as steady as winter, and the person who is still smiling that crooked, loving smile this year, even as they are unsure about locations, histories, appointments, and bills, will be unable to truly converse with meaning or engage in a relationship in a couple of years and will be unable to walk or smile in recognition in ten years and what you will end up hoping, as a friend whose beloved got Alzheimer's at fifty and lived to seventy told me, is that your beloved forgets how to swallow.

I ask the psychiatrist to write a letter for us for Dignitas, just in case we need it, stating that Brian's of sound mind and understands his decision. Brian explains that he needs to be high functioning cognitively to arrange for an assisted suicide. (We call it assisted, because we have not yet gotten used to the Dignitas phrase "accompanied suicide," which sounds to me like an orchestra will be standing by.) It seems quite clear to me that he is of sound mind and he does understand the decision. The psychiatrist doesn't argue or address the subject of his state of mind at all.

She does say, hand to anxious mouth, "Do I have to answer that question now?"

I back off. I say that she does not have to answer now but that she will have to answer soon, because we will be asking her for that letter soon. We all fall silent and then she is half out of her seat, with Maria von Trapp–like enthusiasm, telling us that we should plan for good times and seek out joyful activities. She lifts her hands over her head. She mentions European vacations, trips to beautiful lakes. She says the word *joy* several times, and Brian and I stare at her. We want joy, we do. We really do. And neither of us thinks that eight years of a steady decline and complete loss of self sounds like joy.

When we get home, Brian says, I don't think this will work out. She's not on our team. I agree.

Brian breaks up with the psychiatrist by text. Over the next few days, she texts him, trying to get him to come to her office for closure. I get it. I might have done the same thing. I don't want Brian to go to see this person, because I'm afraid she will upset or confuse him with more talk of a river-barge holiday or the possibility of a cure in his lifetime. (Even on the Alzheimer's websites, the *most* encouraging news lately: phone apps to help you organize or find the Alzheimer's patient. All the recent major failed clinical trials are described as *very helpful in the fight against Alzheimer's*.) I suppose the psychiatrist might get Brian to change his mind, but I doubt it. I don't think *I* could get him to change his mind.

He feels bad for the psychiatrist. He says, I see I've upset her, which inclines him to go see her, and he goes out for a walk. He comes back and says, She's not on our team.

In the end, about as close to the end as we can manage, the psychiatrist does write a short letter for Dignitas.

9/21/19

To whom it may concern,

I am writing at the request of Mr. Brian Ameche, d.o.b. 6/19/53. Mr. Ameche had been under my psychiatric care from 1/22/18 until recently terminating on 9/9/19.

I can document that he was not psychotic, thought disordered, depressed, or suicidal during the time that I was treating him.

Sincerely,

The letter, attesting to Brian's sound mind and the absence of psychosis or thought disorder or suicidality, is not helpful enough; even the Swiss can tell that the doctor is saying as little as possible. Brian texts the psychiatrist one more time for a stronger letter and she does send one. Not much stronger, but she's thrown in a few positive adjectives about his state of mind and made it clear that he has . . . discernment.

I have to send Dignitas the neurologist's written report about Brian's MRI, and it changes everything for the worse, but not because of the content. The problem is that in the upper right-hand corner it says: *Reason for exam: major depressive episode, with current active depression episode.* Brian never suffered from depression and never received treatment of any kind for depression. Neither of us would care, but Dignitas's website makes it very clear that they are not in the business of helping the clinically depressed commit suicide. Heidi of Dignitas, our contact person, has seen the report and already said as much. I do my best to explain to Heidi that the neurologist is wrong. Heidi says, essentially: That may be. Do better or we cannot help you.

I call the neurologist's office the next day and have a short talk with the doctor, who says, Well, I had to say something for why I asked for the MRI, and I knew he was seeing a psychiatrist. It's not important, Amy.

I try to explain that it *is* important without telling her that Dignitas will not accept Brian's application if they see the word *depression*. I ask her if she would change the reason given on the form for ordering the MRI to the more accurate *cognitive difficulties.* She says, It's not important, and hangs up.

I call again the next day and the neurologist doesn't take my call or return it. I get her administrator, who immediately throws herself between the neurologist and me, which I respect, in theory, saying that if Brian and I want to discuss the report, we can make an appointment. I make the appointment, for a month later, and think of it as the Hail Mary appointment: We'll only keep it if every single other thing has failed. I've discovered that, having been a resilient and determined person (perhaps not as much as my husband but still), I now find getting a no, from a person or the universe, is almost unbearable. It destroys my day and more.

• • •

In a few days, we get an email from Heidi at Dignitas in response to everything I've sent her, arranging for our first phone call. I am hopeful and nervous. Brian makes himself a cup of coffee and sits at our kitchen island, calm and ready. I never saw him play football, but I know a goddamn game face when I see one. It's impressive.

If Heidi were a Jew or an Italian from New York, she would be screaming at me. (For this phone call, we have given up the pretense that Brian is handling all of this correspondence on his own, as would a man with . . . discernment.) Heidi asks to speak to me as soon as she's done with the pleasantries with Brian:

"How are you feeling, Mr. Ameche?"

"Pretty good, all things considered."

"That's good to hear, Mr. Ameche."

If Heidi were one of my own relatives, she would not be speaking in a low, emphatic voice; she would be *geshrei*-ing, and what she would be *geshrei*-ing is:

Whaddaya, deaf? You send me this fakakta report and right up there, at the top, what does it say? I'm asking you, young lady, what does it say?! It says, reason for exam: major depressive episode. No good. Are you listening, Amele? THIS IS NO GOOD.

This MRI report, that's your problem. Here's what you gotta do. (At this point, my relative would be knocking whatever I was holding—cup, spoon, or newspaper—out of my hand.) *By us, Alzheimer's is a psychiatric disease. What you gotta get is a proper assessment—not some lukewarm letter, a proper report—is what I'm saying from a proper psychiatrist. You know who we revere here in*

Switzerland? Freud! Get yourself a Dr. Freud and get us a nice long report.
You don't got all day. Until we hear from Dr. Freud, we're not moving a
muscle. And if we don't hear from him, you won't be hearing from us. All
right? All right.

I get off the phone and Brian looks at me dubiously. I have been on the phone, silently sitting and blinking and nodding, for several minutes.

"It's okay," I say. "We just need a better psychiatric report."

"Sure," he says, going back to watching the news.

Brian keeps watching the news and I make dinner. It's disgusting. Having always been a competent and sometimes a very good cook, I am now like any other bad, beleaguered cook. I am often dismayed and surprised by what appears in the pan or the pot. Things that are broiled burn. Things that are sautéed cling and drown. Nothing tastes right. Almost everything is too salty, too oily, or tastes like metal. About once a week, I just throw the whole meal out and we have pizza and a salad or I make sandwiches. I feel that I'm concentrating, but I never am. I have scraped dinner into the garbage again when Donna, Brian's mindfulness/meditation teacher, calls to see how he's doing, since he missed the last class of his meditation course (right day, wrong time). His face lights up and I go into another room. A half hour later, he's off the phone and in an excellent mood. I suggest that he call her back ("How about now," I say, and slide his phone toward him) and see if she'll be his new therapist. He does and she will and God bless her, may she be inscribed in the Book of Life.

A colleague says, "I hear she's flaky." I don't give a damn. I don't care if Donna wears a saffron robe and juggles rose-quartz crystals (she doesn't). Brian leaves every session with Donna with a little spring in his step.

After about two months of twice-a-week meetings with Donna, Brian says that he'd like me to join him.

"For couples therapy?" I say.

Brian thinks over why he wants me to come.

"Sure. And because lots of the stuff we discuss, I don't remember after. You could help me remember."

I say yes immediately. I don't want to do this. We have been in couples therapy, he and I, lots. We had a wonderful old lady who seemed to love us both. Be quiet, she'd tell me, putting up her hand like a crossing guard. It's not your turn. And you, she'd say to Brian, pay attention, this part is important. She told him to stop being a selfish baby and she told me to stop being so hard on him. She said to him, You *chose* her, this woman who doesn't wait on you hand and foot. And just as I was about to say, I actually do, pretty much, wait on him hand and foot, she'd cock a dyed eyebrow in my direction. You *chose* him, you chose the opera and the red sauce, not the white wine and the gloom, at which point she'd cackle and Brian and I would laugh, pleased with all of us. We were mad for her and put her on retainer, in effect, after our first session, a year before we married. We kept up with her, on and off, until a few years ago, when it seemed once more that we had things in hand.

Once, many years ago, Brian was having a couple of bad,

sulky weeks and I wasn't sure why, and I was so mad at him I said that I thought he must be having an affair. He stared at me openmouthed, and then he said, "I'm not having an affair, I'm just being a prick." Then he handed me his phone and said, Call Rachel. We can go see her and then after we can go to Tre Scalini. In the car, he said, Who am I having an affair with? I couldn't think of who it might be, and then the storm was over but we went anyway and also to Tre Scalini, because Brian loved their early-Seventies Italian restaurant vibe and their good Bolognese sauce and their mediocre anti-pasto plates—and he felt about a meal in a restaurant the way people feel about money and good health: always better to have it.

Call me anytime, Rachel had said cheerfully at our last session, five years ago. In 2019, Rachel called me. She'd heard from a patient who was a friend of mine that Brian had Alzheimer's and was going to Dignitas. Just come to my apartment, please, she said.

When I get there, I ring the doorbell many times and finally she appears: thin and distracted. "Oh," she says, "I wasn't sure it was the doorbell." Her house is a shrine to psychoanalytic theory, Marimekko, and mid-century tchotchkes from all over the world, and she guides me to a worn sofa.

She tells me that although she's told her patients she has a medical condition and will be retiring soon, she actually has Alzheimer's and hopes she can refer some patients to me. She can't find the patients' names, and we sit down and she says: I heard about you and Brian. I'm hoping, I can, y'know, get on board with the two of you. She describes the way the three of us could travel to Sweden. Switzerland, I say, and I tell her that that's not the way it works, that it's quite a long process of application. She looks disappointed.

"Do you know I have Alzheimer's?" she says.

"Yes, I do."

"How do you know that? Who told you?"

I don't mention the visit (or the next or the next) to Brian. I tell Rachel that I will have to be out of touch for a while (because Brian and I are working on getting to Zurich and I know I cannot shepherd him and then her). She tells me that her lawyer is on her side and that she thinks maybe he can help her get to Sweden. Switzerland. I say encouraging things about her lawyer, who sounds like a nice man, and I say, repeatedly, that I hope she talks to her daughters about how she's feeling. "You mean about my hip," she says. I say no, I mean her forgetfulness. "Well, they don't need to know," she says. "You know, Amy. You can take care of it."

I encourage her, again, to talk to her daughters about her concerns and I know that everything I am saying is pointless. Finally, I ask for her daughters' phone numbers, and Rachel cannot or will not give the numbers to me. She winds up in the care of one of her daughters, and she does not get to Dignitas, because that window probably closed two years earlier, and she will spend the rest of her life in a memory-care unit, and the best outcome I can hope for is that she dies soon. She does not die very soon and when we talk next, she is in the memory-care unit and she says, Something very strange is going on here, please come get me.

Birdseed

One day, after breakfast, Brian says, "I should get bird-seed. We don't have any. I put birdseed out all year round, and then a few weeks ago there were bugs in the seed and so I stopped for a couple of weeks."

"You stopped for a year," I say, and I think, What in Jesus's name is wrong with you, Amy? Who cares?

Obviously I do, because I wish to make the point that the birds have suffered and that even though the bugs-in-the-seed problem was bad (and it was gross: Winged bugs flew out like a horror movie), he didn't deal with it for almost two years, *in fact*. I am, apparently, committed to telling him it was more than two weeks. Brian's in charge of all things avian, and I've affronted him by telling him that he hasn't taken care of the birds. I try hard not to say things like this, but every once in a while my need to prove a point, such a base and unattractive need, rises up and I meet it by telling him things that he doesn't need to hear. I'm ashamed of myself, but then Brian turns on me and says that he can't understand why he is being "grilled" about birdseed. He gets a little loud and very irritable and he leaves abruptly to go fishing and I'm glad, not only because he's gone but since he yelled at me, quite unfairly (you could say that I was pressing the point about the unfed birds, but I wasn't *grilling* him), I don't feel ashamed anymore.

Days later, we are in Donna's office, still talking about bird-seed, after a fashion. Brian sees the birds outside Donna's win-dow and says, I should get some birdseed. I nod.

We are there for something like couples therapy. It looks like couples therapy, since we are sitting next to each other, facing her, in a small room with beige carpeting and we look at each other at intervals, fondly and nervously. A couple of times my eyes well up with tears. It's not like couples therapy, because neither of us has the hope that the other will change. Whoever Brian is now is who he's going to be for as long as our life together lasts. Then I think, well, that's true of most couples therapy, really, although it's not usually how I open the first session when I'm the therapist.

In November 2019, in Donna's office, months after the diag-nosis but before the acceptance from Dignitas, Brian says, I think I'd like to go on one last vacation before I die.

Donna (she'd been leading him toward a discussion of ways he can show me support): Ah. A vacation.

Me (inside voice): *Are you fucking kidding me? Arrange a trip? Now? And where? Someplace we've been and loved, which will now be some half-baked, propped-up version of the real thing? Some new place that I will help you negotiate while you chafe at my attention and wander off to the We Never Close Bar in some foreign city, with nothing but a pocketful of euros and your friendly grin?*

Me (outside voice): Oh. A vacation. Sure. Yes.

By the time we get home, I'm hoping that he will have forgotten the big vacation. I ask him if maybe he wants a little holiday. I don't mention a big holiday. A week ago, Great Wayne mentioned Brian might like one last big fishing trip and that I could, after all, stay at a motel in New Jersey while Brian fished for false albacore. I see that Wayne knows something about fishing and, like most men who like to fish, he has a real, if casual, affection for other men who fish. He's *sympathetic* to the need to fish. Because it's Wayne, I make calls to five different fishing guides in Jersey. It's early November and it's turned cold. No one will go. I tell Wayne I called five different fishing guides, because I don't want him to think that I don't care about my husband's happiness. I understand that all happiness is fleeting, but I see now that there is fleeting and then there is the true and wall-like impossibility of ever experiencing this kind of happiness again, even once, even next week, let alone a year from now. Doors are closing around us, all the time. I reluctantly and hopefully call three more guides, working in the Carolinas. (And I tell Wayne about them, too.)

I have failed Brian.

. . .

And his doctors have failed him, including his internist, Good Time Charlie, the doctor who hates bad news. When Brian came to him a few years before, in 2016, complaining about his memory, GTC was all reassurance and Brian came home and told me so.

When we went to him for our B-12 discussion, Good Time Charlie was, as always, pleased to see Brian and didn't say anything about seeing me. He looked at the referral from the neurologist and said, So, vitamin B-12. He said that B-12 used to be given by injection, that injection had been the gold standard, but—good news—not anymore. He said Brian should take B-12 in a massive dose, sublingually (dissolving under the tongue), and he should take it for the rest of his life. Charlie explains that he's ordering a second, superior B-12 test, which will reveal, he hopes, another possible cause of the B-12 deficiency, atrophic gastritis, in which the stomach lining has thinned and absorption is a problem. He looks at us pleasantly and half-rises out of his seat. I see that we are dismissed, and I see that Brian has no wish for further discussion.

Brian's blood test comes back normal, and I'm glad and I'm still angry and puzzled about the last meeting and I leave a voicemail for Charlie.

He calls me a few days later and I tell him that I can't understand why in the course of our meeting he never asked about the referral from the neurologist or Brian's cognitive issues. He stammers and says that he assumed the referral was for headaches.

WHAT HEADACHES? I tell Charlie that if he looks at Brian's chart, he will see that Brian has barely ever had a headache in his life.

Charlie says, "Okay," like a fourteen-year-old boy, mulish and nervous.

"What does that mean? Does this seem okay to you? Okay that you had no interest in why a longtime patient was being referred by a neurologist? What's okay about that?"

"Okay," he says.

"It is not okay," I say.

The End of the Guilford Fair

The end of the Guilford Fair was a nightmare. The only thing that would have made it worse would have been if the twins were with us, but Brian got through the ice cream purchases and the funhouse with them and now they've gone home with their parents. September rolling in, MRI behind us, we had managed to slide and swerve around the rising weeds of Brian's dementia when they sprang up near the twins.

Once a week, for the last year, since retirement, Brian would pick the girls up from school or, in the summer, from camp. This summer, he went to get them at camp and couldn't find them. Their mother and I waited in my driveway. I called his phone, over and over. After almost an hour, I got in my car to go find them all and called him one more time from the road and reached him. (We had as many fights about his phone as about all other things combined; the more difficult it became for him to use it, the more he rejected it, carrying it in case he needed it but turning the ringer off all day.) He sounded ragged, breathing hard. He said that he couldn't find the room they were in and, also, they had been running around somewhere. Then he said that they were crying and everyone was upset. It was like talking to a man stranded by the side of the road, watching the car he'd just tumbled out of explode. I asked him if he needed me to come get him. He said no, that he'd be coming home soon, with the twins.

I fish in their memories occasionally, but neither of the twins seems to remember this incident. Eden remembers Babu playing checkers in a new "crazy" way, but she has sorted this as a memory of his being silly on purpose. That day he came late to pick them up, couldn't find them at Guilford Lakes School, and they shouted at him and he shouted at them seems to have disappeared, gone below the surface.

My daughter and I spent family dinner that night smoothing things over. Brian swore, in front of us all, hand to God, that he did not say to them, "I will never pick you up again." (Although I am sure he did say that. When the emails from his book club got overwhelming, when the online exchanges about fishing plans were too much for him, he'd say angrily, This is crazy. I won't do this again.) Brian assured the girls that of course he would be happy to pick them up, anytime. (He never did it again without me.) Tears were dried. Hugs were had. They sat in his lap and ate most of his potato chips. And by the time we all went to the Guilford Fair two months later, the people who didn't know about Brian's Alzheimer's and our hopes and plans for Dignitas were the grandchildren and most of our friends, the people we wished to protect and be protected from.

At Connecticut small-town fairs, giant fields are turned into parking lots for thousands of Subarus and Hondas. Old men in neon vests and stoned teenagers direct you to spaces. Rows and rows of shimmering, sunbaked cars faced us, and most of the parking-space pointers had now gone home. I looked left, Brian looked right, and then he was gone. He had decided to explore other, farther rows. (It will not surprise you to read that we were in the wrong lot entirely. Our lot was beside a different, more dilapidated white farmhouse, one field away.) I phoned him every couple of minutes. I began to cry. I pictured us reunited many hours later, when the fair closed, Brian brought to me by Guilford Fair security (slightly beefier versions of the parking-space pointers), humiliated and furious.

Instead, after forty minutes during which tears and sweat ran from my face to my feet, I reached Brian on the phone and he told me where he was—Just standing by the llamas, darling—and I ran to him, slowing down before he saw me, so I didn't seem alarmed. I was so frightened and anxious, I could hardly speak. I could not stop hugging him. Brian suggested we walk down to the road, from back to front this time, and then look for a place to perch, for an aerial view. We did and I saw the other lot. We found our car. I drove us home and Brian made himself a cheese plate and watched the news while I took a shower and recovered from the second panic attack of my life.

Thursday, November 14, 2019, Stony Creek

Moonlight in Vermont

By late November, there's frost and I live with panic. Thanksgiving is nearly here. The clock is ticking, which doesn't describe it. The ticking clock is on the only door through which I can help my husband walk. Dignitas, the only door in the world for us, is closing and locking in front of me. Sometimes I go to my office to pace and then to cry. I ask everyone I can stand to ask if they know someone who might help us; mostly I don't ask, because I can't take it.

In one session, Donna, who has steadily supported Brian as he makes his peace with choosing to end his life and has encouraged me to cry when needed and not give up, suggests we call an old friend of hers, Dr. Bornstrom. I can't quite figure out what he does: actual end-of-life activities, turkey-brining bag and Party City helium tank, which I've just read all about on a New Zealand website while sitting in the parking lot of Donna's office. Five minutes ago, I didn't know anything about this technique and now I have a fairly complete grasp on it. All of the advice is sensible and terrifying and I am pretty sure that I can't do it and Brian won't have it. I am still searching for whoever it is, the person who will help us, who will help us do whatever needs to be done.

While Brian is in the restroom, Donna asks me if he might like to go to Vermont and have a psychedelic pre-death trip. She says that psilocybin has been shown to reduce people's fears about their impending death, helping them better embrace their limited time on earth and be at peace with their death. It sounds like a good thing and I say no. I don't think I can do it, which is not the right place to stand on this, and all the way driving home I worry that in my selfishness and fear and aversion to psychedelic drugs (when I was in high school, the three boys in our little group got so high once or twice a week that they were immobile, tripping the day away. I made apple fritters in the kitchen of whoever's mother wasn't home and I pulled the blankets up around the boys before I left) I am depriving Brian of something that could help, could even be an exceptional experience. (He tripped a few times in college and after and seems to have suffered no effects at all, aside from still getting very lost in any place that *isn't* the wilderness.) In the driveway, I tell Brian that this psychedelic experience is available to him and that we can go to Vermont anytime. Brian takes my hand. I'm sad, he says, and I'm still kinda angry, he says, but I'm not afraid. We don't have to schlep to Vermont.

Fall 2019, Stony Creek

We are waiting on Dignitas. Brian dictated his bio for them:

Biographical statement for Brian Ameche

I was born in Kenosha, Wisconsin, the son of first-generation, working-class Italian-American high school sweethearts. My father became a well-known college football player and then a professional athlete and he and my mother had five children (me, my three brothers, and two sisters) by the time they were 25. Eventually, there were six children, of whom I am the eldest. My youngest brother, Paul, died at 20 and we all miss him still.

    We moved four or five times in my childhood

and I spent most of my adolescence in Philadelphia, Pennsylvania, and went to private school there. I was on the wrestling, lacrosse, and football teams and was captain of all three teams through high school. I was recruited by Yale University, to play varsity football there for four years. As with many football players, my doctors have suggested that my years of hard contact on the football field may have led to my dementing disease.

I took some time off before graduate school and worked as a guide (hiking, climbing, fishing) in Colorado for a year. I'm still an avid fly fisherman and had hoped to do some guiding and instructing in my retirement.

Always drawn to design, construction, and visual art, I went to the University of Minnesota and got my Master's in Architecture. I (like my father) married my high school sweetheart and we returned to New Haven, Connecticut, where I began my architectural career. In the course of the past almost-forty years, I have designed public housing projects (some of my best work), the women's athletic fields at Yale, a country club, a leading assisted-living facility, apartment buildings, corporate offices, and a wonderful Girl Scout camp. I loved designing and would be doing it still, if not for Alzheimer's.

In my early fifties, my marriage ended. I met and fell in love with Amy, and we married, twelve years ago, with our friends and my family and her three wonderful children around us. We have built

a great and happy life together and I am more
sorry than I can say that Alzheimer's is putting an
end to that.

Ben A. Ande

I tweak it a little and read it back to him. He makes a few
more changes and gives it back to me. I make all the changes
he wants, and he drops a line about his father winning the
Heisman Trophy when I say, Jesus Christ, darling, they're
Swiss. They don't care. Done. We have scones and coffee (and
bacon and eggs for him) to sort of celebrate. Dignitas is pretty
much my job now. We have dinners, we have the kids, I have
some version of work, he has stained glass and therapy and
the gym, to which I will be driving him by October. Brian is
content, as far as that goes, to check in with me every few days
regarding our Dignitas application process and offer encour-
agement. Occasionally, when we hit a speed bump of which
he's aware, he says: This is crazy. It's *my* life, I should get to
decide how to end it. Most days, he seems to feel that I've got
the situation well in hand, that the end is coming too soon,
certainly, but not right around the corner, not before we can
do sushi and a movie many more times and that nothing bad
will happen in the process, which will unfold as we expect.
This is not true, that nothing bad will happen, and therefore
not comforting to me. It leaves me quite alone with reality, but
the way he feels is exactly what I want for him.

Often, in the morning, he puts his hand on me and says,
Today, I feel pretty good. Sometimes he says, I feel like my
memory is about 90 percent. I say that's great. Some mornings, he says, I think I'll start driving to the gym again, and we

agree, as we do every time, that a reasonable compromise is that I'll drive him or our son-in-law, Corey, will drive him to the gym (twenty-five minutes away) but that he can drive to the stained-glass studio, six minutes away (straight up the road and turn right at the Chowder Pot).

To stained glass, today at 11:00.

Drive up the road past Stop and Shop, TURN RIGHT at the giant lobster.

Jayne's studio is on the left, at Apple Orchard Gallery.

And I draw a heart.

This one time, Brian leaves to work on his last stained-glass project (a sunset or a sunrise) and comes back in three minutes. I forgot how to go, he says, and it is his bravery in saying so, getting the directions from me and going out again, that levels me. This man? This is the one that has to shuffle off this mortal coil? Every morning, as soon as Brian leaves our bedroom, I cry, furiously. I mentally review all the people— not even bad people, just people I happen to know—who should have to die instead of him.

A Little Help

At the same time that we are trying to check all the boxes for Dignitas, I take seriously their slow and careful approach and their underlining that *no* is a definite possibility. I'm trying to create Plan B, according to Brian's directives, in which I get him a completely painless and lethal dose of something he can drink—no injections—while the kids gather round and I hold his hand. (I've read up, and on top of all that, I will have to make it look like I'm out at the movies or taking a long walk while he's dying from his lethal dose, and that strikes me, a lover of English mysteries, as very suspicious behavior. How many wives leave a husband with Alzheimer's on his own for the evening while they pop off to a movie or take a long stroll through the marsh?)

• • •

While Brian is out walking the Trolley Trail, a pretty path through the marshes, I'm making sausage and peppers wrapped in eggs for Jack, my dear friend and former student, who prides himself on being handy, helpful, canny, and crafty, with the long-lashed, round, and guileless eyes and pink cheeks that canny and crafty call for. Jack is, maybe, my best bet for advice on Plan B. Jack has fixed things around the house, fixed stairs and cabinets for our friends, and researched for me. I often make him breakfast, suggest things to read, and edit his writing. It sounds much more transactional than it is. I would cook for him anyway. He would fix my wobbly table anyway. It's a little embarrassing (for me, maybe for him) but we just love each other; we are a happy match of dovetailing foibles and compatible personalities, quirks, and amusements, forty years apart. Brian is very fond of Jack. Since Alzheimer's, for Brian, trust matters even more than fond, and he also trusts Jack. (Brian's decided that our electrician, the nicest and most competent of men, is "shirking," is "not doing things properly." The man has saved our house over and over for a decade and he's come to our house multiple times in the last three months because Brian chose to redo, reconnect, or disconnect some crucial bit of wiring.)

I make coffee for Jack and me, one eye on the clock. (Brian is a certain kind of CEO for this project: He doesn't want to participate in discussions below his pay grade, he doesn't want to overhear troubling or puzzling discussions, he doesn't want any bad news, he doesn't want any unsolved problems presented, and regular progress reports are appreciated. No meeting should last more than ten minutes.) I'd told Jack about Brian's diagnosis a couple of weeks ago and tried to

finish my sentences between gulping tears. I couldn't understand why I cried nonstop during these phone calls. I was sure
that Brian had Alzheimer's before the MRI; I'd thought, It's
not a *surprise*. But it was a surprise the way every bad thing,
even as you see the flames in the distance, even as the terrible
thing is upon you, breathing in your ear, hammering on your
narrow bones, is still a surprise.

I begin with a rant about the American healthcare system,
our refusal to let people die a dignified and comfortable death,
the money made off suffering, the doctors unable to face their
limits and meet the needs of their patients. Jack listens and
eats. I swear constantly and unimaginatively.

"Nobody can talk about it," I say. "Nobody seems to know
what they're doing. There is literally no treatment. The most
advanced Alzheimer's research in the world says: Eat fucking
blueberries. Get enough fucking sleep."

Jack nods.

Brian comes home and they both have more breakfast
and I think that sexism will exist as long as women give birth,
because the two of them, the young man and the not-young
man, and me, as well, are all happy as can be with them sitting
like paying customers and me turning bacon, toasting bread,
and filling mugs.

A few days later, Jack's in my office, while Brian is at the stained-
glass studio. I want to think out loud. I lie on my couch, with
my hand over my eyes, the way I do when I'm trying to plot
a scene for a novel, and Jack paces and then sits in my armchair. I've looked up how much pentobarbital we'd need. The

amount is buried in some document for Exit International or Dignitas, but I unearth it (and forget it, twice, and unearth it again—I think Brian's Alzheimer's is destroying my memory) and finally write the amount, *20 GRAMS*, on an index card. He's got to take an anti-emetic, I say, so he won't throw it all up. Then the stuff goes in a blender, to make a smoothie, and I have to wear gloves if I help at all, so it's only Brian's finger-prints on it. I say, It's a crime, Jack.

I know that I want my children with us and I know that if we do this, they would want to plant themselves by my side, but I cannot bear to have any of them, parents all, face any legal consequences. I think that maybe they would come over after, and I can't imagine where they would all be waiting, or what happens after. I cannot imagine this, and I close my eyes and focus on the smallest, most useless details—what room, what time of day—repeatedly. Jack leaves, quietly.

I research at the public library. *Not* on the phone, *not* on my laptop. The internet tells me, again and again, not to search anything from my own computer and that if I need to know something, call, don't text, and don't use my own laptop. I understand that if there were ever to be a real investigation, dunking my laptop into a barrel of acid won't stop the police from finding my search history, if they know how to look for it. I research fentanyl, and every website confirms that it's fifty to one hundred times stronger than morphine. For legit purposes, people receive it in a patch or an IV and get the steady release of extremely low doses. What's not promising: The street version's cooked in some guy's lab, made into a powder or eye drops or nasal spray or pills or blotter paper, and although I am not current with the street drug circle, I'm pretty sure that it's still true that the more valuable the stuff, the more likely it is not to be what your dealer says it is. The consequences of lying are negligible; if the stuff is lethally bad, the customer is dead. Problem solved. If it's just not pure or even effective, the customer can complain but can't sue and is unlikely to kill the dealer. (I assume that if I was the kind of customer who was likely to kill the dealer, said dealer would have taken precautions.) So, even if I, swanning to the buy in my clogs and Madewell jeans, could get fenty, it might not be fentanyl at all, and even if it was fenty, Brian might experience distressing confusion, agitation, and seizures before his death. I can't get clear about how long the stuff takes to act, because most of the fenty overdoses recorded are not suicides by large, middle-aged men. Because there were a lot of said overdoses in the last couple of years, fenty is hard to get and therefore hard to buy. No fenty.

I do a close read on Exit International's website. I try not to get distracted by the Sarco, a person-size capsule for the suicide of the future, designed by Philip Nitschke and a Dutch designer: *Where Art Meets Its End . . . The concept of a capsule that could produce a rapid decrease in oxygen level, while maintaining a low CO_2 level (the conditions for a peaceful, even euphoric death), led to Sarco's development. Is it art or . . . ? The elegant design was intended to suggest a sense of occasion: of travel to a "new destination," and to dispel the "yuk" factor.*

I can't.

· · ·

I dig into our materials from Dignitas, now that we are at least members and possible candidates. I dismiss a bunch of other options: The turkey-brining bag with helium tube, which is described as painless and looks monstrous. Phenobarbital gotten from not-too-fussy veterinarians in Mexico (or closer to home, if you can find a vet who will believe you have a horse you wish to put down, all by your lonesome). But sodium pentobarbital, a common, once very popular barbiturate and central-nervous-system depressant, is the thing. An overdose will certainly kill you and it will kill you painlessly; in less than a minute, you fall into a light sleep, in ten minutes, a deep sleep. In twenty, the heart stops. The lethal dose of sodium pentobarbital is roughly one gram per ten pounds. For Brian, it would take at least twenty grams to be sure. This is a fuckton of a controlled substance. Abbott Labs stopped making it in 1999. Because it is what's used for lethal injections for executions in America, drug companies are not elbowing one another out of the way to produce a tightly controlled substance with lots of bad press. When the pills are made, they are made in fifty- or one-hundred-milligram tablets. We'd need five hundred. I call our few doctor friends for help. With real kindness, they make it clear that getting pentobarbital is (1) not their jam and (2) really really hard to do. One said, This (a self-administered suicide dose) is something that usually fails. Another, older friend said, Is Brian really sure about this? If it was me, I'd just be selfish and live as much life as I could and rely on my wife to take care of me to the end. I thought that was probably true.

I make a last call and this doctor friend, who already

knows Brian's diagnosis, who has already sat with me while I sobbed over multiple coffees, says to me, "So, I guess you're saying you need a barbiturate for sleeping because Ambien isn't enough for your insomnia." And I'm late for my cue but I do manage to stumble through my line. I agree that my insomnia is an intractable bitch and only sodium pentobarbital (words I didn't even know three weeks ago) would help. "Well, then," the doctor says, "I'll prescribe sodium pentobarbital. Be very careful with it." I am enormously grateful, but it will come to nothing. I hand the scrip to the pharmacist at CVS, who does not call the police or the FBI or even the manager. She looks at it and makes a phone call and I loiter near the feminine-hygiene products until she jerks her head and I go to the pickup area.

"I put in the order," she says, and I can hear now that she has a German accent. "I wouldn't count on it. Is very hard to get."

"But it's legal," I say, in my Helpy Helperpants way, telling the woman things she knows.

"Yes, but the distribution of it in America is . . . not good. Call me in ten days."

I wait the ten days and reach the pharmacist.

No go.

"You might try Walgreens," she says. "They use a different distribution system. I will never be able to get this for you."

I call Walgreens and the pharmacist there says instantly, Nope. I'll never be able to get this for you.

No go.

. . .

I could try to order sodium pentobarbital from Germany or Denmark or China, where they still make and distribute the stuff, but the internet tells me that customs does random drug screening on packages. I could claim that I didn't know who sent it, and my color and age might protect me, but even if I didn't go to jail, I still wouldn't have the sodium pentobarbital and Brian would still have Alzheimer's, worse than he does today, and I would have failed him. I picture the police at my doorstep, interviewing me and walking into the TV room to interview Brian.

I ask Jack about the dark web, and Jack tries to tell me.

"Well, basically it's like Yelp. The dark web is this tiny part of the deep web, where you have these encrypted sites that require specific software to access. But once you're in, it's almost like a new-age version of the classifieds, but better, because vendors have reviews. The better their reviews, the more likely you'll actually get what you're buying. They're paid in Bitcoin. It's a file stored in a digital wallet. You can pay for it with a credit card or through a wire transfer, or trade for it with other goods, and then you buy stuff with it."

Sure.

"Basically, you set up your computer to do some really complex sums, and occasionally a Bitcoin will pop out. But at this point, it's so complex, even with a really powerful computer it could be years before you get a hit."

Sure.

I tell Jack he's been very helpful. I study up, right on the internet, about blockchains and blenders and discover one morning that the FBI has just shut down the dark-web marketplace and shut down one of the biggest vendor-review sites and a few blenders, to boot. The dark-web community is not, according to the article, comfortable.

Done with that.

I turn to our local casino to brighten our days, because Brian has been a happy and, I think, competent blackjack player since I've known him. I don't know anything about gambling; I know that I think it's idiotic. Dog races, horse races, side bets, slot machines, baccarat, and blackjack—it seems a lot like throwing money out the window, but that's because I do not get the thrill of the chase. Brian does. I noodle around the Mohegan Sun website and read this:

ASPIRE LUXURY SUITE

Each Aspire Luxury King Suite features up to 1,145 square feet of luxurious furnishings including a bedroom with plush King bed, a living room featuring a pull-out sofa and walk-in closet with automatic lighting. A spacious bathroom with a Jacuzzi and 1/2 bath along with high-end amenities round out this upscale experience.

I used to write copy. My boss told me: If you gotta say it's upscale, it ain't. My boss said, It's like that guy who tells you he's funny.

I read the description aloud to Brian. He shrugs.

"You could play blackjack," I say. I don't know if he can still play blackjack.

"Do you want to see a picture of the room?" I say.

It's just what I expect, a banal version of grand, with tufted carpeting and a polyester bedspread, and it's still a thousand dollars a night. We will be spending money we don't have. I can't write, and Brian is suddenly retired, three years ahead of schedule but still, he could gamble a little and get a decent steak. We'll sit in some plushy chairs in a room with low lighting and scented air while he has a club soda with many slices of lime and I drink half a martini and then he'll go play blackjack. I'll people-watch while he wins and loses and maybe wins five hundred dollars after a couple of hours. I take out my credit card. I want his face to light up, as it used to over so many things. Lighting up, that two-handed delight: Let's get both kinds of cheesecake, go to Le Marche for a month when we retire, build a grape arbor—hell, open a winery!—drive to Montreal, stay in bed all morning, watch *The Lady Vanishes* this weekend. That's what I miss.

This disinterested dusk is hard.

He's not toying with me. This is not a marital game of who-gets-what/fair-is-fair. (We have not been bean counters, mostly. I'm a bean-counting bitch about the way Italian food dominates every other cuisine in our house and the way barbecue sauce is counted as a basic food group, for all the good it does me. My mother-in-law once sent us a box of cured meats as an anniversary present. Ten pounds of cured meats and three barbecue sauces.) Brian's not performing lack of interest in the casino to get me back on board with a holiday in Florence or Paris and then maybe compromising with a long weekend in Manhattan. He's not doing anything that has anything to do with me. The casino doesn't appeal; the idea of gambling, the wish to win or chase, has faded. Practicing hours of blackjack on his laptop as he used to, getting ready for an evening of cards with a dealer and other players, seems a lifetime ago. Brian never brings up the idea of a holiday again.

All fall, I find myself making suggestions for trips I don't want to take: Florence and Paris, or one or the other—they could be lovely in late November, I say (which is not what I think; I think it will be beyond melancholy and I will regret that I don't drink heavily). I remind him of the beach resort we went to twice, each time one of my parents died. He loved it and I remind him of all the things he loved about it: the private beach we got dropped off upon and frolicked about upon for a few hours, naked and too old to be naked and still happy about it, like extras in a Fellini movie. The big afternoon tea, which allowed us to skip the overpriced lunch, where he could drink two pots of Earl Grey, fill his pockets with cookies, and while away a happy hour. I remind him of the evening when we walked to the little restaurant up the road and the flirtatious waitress, who managed to make both of us feel irresistible. He smiles distantly at all of this. And then I go online to show him some photos of his very favorite hotel in Manhattan and I talk about the morning we had breakfast in the room, took a walk, and came back for another, fancier breakfast, and he shakes his head, the way you do when someone has insisted on reminding you of an unimportant detail.

I have failed him.

Better to Be Lucky

The good days still have sweetness. If I can't fall asleep quickly, I ask Brian if I can spoon him and he lies on his right side and I spoon him and sometimes, like the old days (three years ago), I slide my hand under his T-shirt and take in his amazingly smooth skin and his smell, which hasn't changed: wood and cinnamon. I lie on his shoulder and we watch an incomprehensible Scottish mystery. I fall asleep during a crucial ten minutes and when I wake up Brian tells me why the rocking chair or convertible or chicken coop is covered in blood. We eat a couple of cookies in bed and I point out that there's been a change (not a bad thing but still . . .) in Rachel Maddow's lip gloss and he admires my keen eye and we brush the cookie crumbs onto the floor because no one is watching. I plump my pillow so vigorously, it knocks everything off my nightstand, and he laughs and says that I'm a danger to myself and others. Those moments are all I want. I want a life of this. He sighs and I sigh.

The bad days are pretty much the birdseed moment, all day long. Sometimes it's worse than the bickering over facts or the heavy gloom that descends on him, for which I do not blame him at all but it makes for a dark house. Brian gets an email from an old classmate, asking if he'll arrange a fishing expedition for her and her husband. This was what he hoped to do when he retired—be a fishing guide, like he was in his twenties, when he took rich people out to hike and fish in Colorado. He mulls it over and I keep my mouth shut. At a couple of points, I actually lay my hand over my mouth. He can't do it. He can still fish and he could show someone how to cast, but he can't arrange an expedition and I don't want to. I don't want to help them have a once-in-a-lifetime day of fishing on the Housatonic River. I will be trading emails, making lunches, and trying to backstop Brian every inch of the way. Brian muses out loud for about ten minutes and says, with some sadness, I'll have to decline. He puts on his hat and goes to fish and I am relieved, and I want to run after him and say, We can do it, if you really want to.

All fall, I veer between hand-wringing and grim determination. Rosh Hashanah comes and goes, likewise Yom Kippur, likewise a dinner party at which Brian unexpectedly excels at Celebrities and I feel a fool to have worried at all, likewise our family's own Oktoberfest, in which my son and eldest granddaughter, our number one, Isadora (we were with her the day she was born, a bit too soon, in the middle of

a fix-up-the-new-house visit, and we walked the halls and
fielded calls and hugged and kissed everyone, including the
nurses, did the atheists' version of prayer, and now Brian
calls her Darling, just to be on the safe side), come down from
Rochester, my daughter and my daughter-in-law and our
shining light, little Zora, come up from Brooklyn, and we all
go through a corn maze, with clues, and they get their faces
or pumpkins painted and there is a donkey ride, after which
we all eat an enormous lunch at Bishop's Orchards. I have a
memory of Zora waving from a small train that goes through
a field and Izzy and the twins jumping from bale to bale in a
hay tower. I cannot hold Brian in the picture. I know he went
through the maze. I know he must have gone grinning down
the big slide (there was never a big slide he didn't go down).
I know he must have ordered the grilled corn and the fancy
fries, but I cannot see him in my mind's eye. I cannot see much
of that fall, and only pieces of Thanksgiving or Hanukkah or
Christmas. I know we celebrated them all and I know he was
there and I know, for that matter, that I was there, too, thinking, This will probably be the last, and fearing it would not be,
that I would fail to help him, fail to help him get to Zurich, to
the other side of the river, however we must go. I do remember Christmas because it is smaller than usual, just us and the
kids and grandchildren and I beg off having my sister and her
family, and I hardly care that I am disappointing them all. I
remember it only because there are photos of Brian and me,
him large and grand in his father's jewel-toned silk robe, me,
frowning, in my tatty robe. Sunlight is coming through the
big window behind us and I look like an old woman on a long
train ride, barely sitting up.

Memory Care

The leaves are yellow and red and I'm done reading about dementia (Alzheimer's and the other ones: occipital, the one that makes you blind first, and another one, frontotemporal lobe, which moves faster and sometimes more dramatically with a personality shift, either to great, unshakable sweetness or to aggressive, sometimes-violent outbursts). I'm done reading about ways of ending your life and the laws about that. In the last few weeks, Brian and I have both observed, with something more than interest, that a memory-care unit is being built ten minutes from us. We drive past the construction site all the time and we remark on it, in the ways we do: Brian on the square footage, me, that it looks like a Red Roof Inn. Yesterday, we drove back from the grocery store and I slowed down as we passed it and Brian waved a hand. Drive on.

When Brian's not around, I still sometimes sneak-watch

videos of people with dementia and their loved ones: "Dementia Diaries" and Louis Theroux's 2012 documentary, *Extreme Love: Dementia*. I step into and out of a BBC year-in-the-life series, with three people with dementia. There is one couple I come back to: in their late sixties, early seventies, so blue-eyed and best-foot-forward English they seem to have fallen from a Trollope (Anthony or Joanna) novel of people of a certain class and manner. Christopher's a good-looking, white-haired, sweater-matches-the-eyes nautical type, working with ships for the last ten years, a magistrate before his retirement, and diagnosed seven years ago. There are photos all along the mantels and shelves; twenty years ago, he was gorgeous and carelessly impressive, and I know his now-wife must have fallen for him like a ton of bricks. I imagine that she left her husband, a balding real-estate lawyer. Possibly, her children were upset and never quite got over it, but everyone's pleasant enough during the holidays and there were grandchildren and she was with the love of her life, so quite a happy ending, until Alzheimer's. The wife, keen, loving, and British to the core, says, "And when you were a magistrate, you realized that things were, as you say, passing you by." He chuckles and agrees. She chuckles encouragingly. She says, "And, of course, you never knew who you'd put away or didn't." He chuckles some more, as if to say, Quite right, old girl. I've watched this documentary three times, while emailing one more time to Wisconsin, Connecticut, and Pennsylvania for Brian's various forms (birth certificate, divorce papers, our marriage certificate). Christopher says, punching his fist into his open hand, the gesture that punctuates all of his remarks about life, about pushing forward, about refusing to be stopped or cowed: "You have to keep on, but at some point, you have to decide what you're going to do."

I think he means that at some point in the infinity pool of dementia, you have to decide how long you want to stay. His wife either interprets his remark differently than I do or we share the same interpretation and she rejects it, because she says heartily, That's right, you have to cope. He says, in agreement, but without conviction, Yes, cope.

I love him. A few minutes later, describing the difference between dementia and age-related absentmindedness, she says, grinning furiously, You just forget, don't you (meaning Christopher)? You just get into the car and you forget why you're there, don't you? He's nodding and chuckling. She is in agony and comes close to laughing out loud, saying, to the camera, It is quite shattering at first.

Lifeboat

We still don't have a green light. I sit across from Great Wayne, unable to speak. When I come into his office, in the basement of his house, I usually hurl myself on his couch, as if it's a lifeboat, and I fall into a deep, short nap. (I've seen him once a week since March, when I called for an appointment. After a few sessions, Wayne said, with therapeutic tact: You seem so attentive and attuned to my responses. Perhaps it'd be easier, less work for you, if you lie on the couch—pointing out the super-Freudian, Peruvian-rug-covered couch in the corner. I didn't care if this was what he really thought or if he worried that grief made me incapable of sitting upright. I jumped out of the chair and lay down on the couch, immediately.)

This time, I come in and sit up in Wayne's dumpy armchair, like a pilgrim at whatever artifact—the weeping statue of the Virgin or the scrap of petrified cloth—that believers drag themselves to, and who am I to make remarks about the desperate and terrified? I have contemplated approaching a couple of neurologists I don't know, both with a reputation for mild loopiness, at best. I am still looking for any amenable doctor, neurologist, or psychiatrist who does not recoil at the very sound of Dignitas. I can't find one.

In the past, I would have said that I was heartbroken. These days, I know better what "heartbroken" is and I'm a little ashamed that I used to use it so lightly and foolishly, indulging in my own rich emotional life. What an idiot.

I tell Wayne about everyone I have asked, or hesitated to ask, and every disappointment. I detail the troubles with the various doctors, just to show that I have been trying hard. He pulls his great eyebrows together when I tell him about the neurologist and I hold my breath and think, Oh, may this be the mighty hand, the outstretched arm of justice and mercy I have been looking for. I tell him what we need, a medical letter saying that there is not now, nor was there ever in the past, any evidence of clinical depression in Brian.

I say, If you think that a long life is of great value just because it is our only time here on earth, or because you appreciate what God has allotted you, or because there might be the possibility of treatment or cure for whatever ails you within your lifetime, if only the lifetime is long enough—your view will be different than mine. If you are the kind of person who sees death as the enemy and continued life itself as a victory, no matter how lonely, painful, or disabled that life may be, who feels that quality of life is only one slim tree in a big forest, one arguable virtue in the big battle—your view is different than mine, and different than Brian's.

My husband is guided by three principles, I tell Wayne:

Take yes for an answer.

Better to ask forgiveness than permission.

And—for better and worse—if it looks like a fight, throw the first punch.

Back in the day, visiting Harvard while playing football for Yale, Brian was jumped in a stairwell by three Harvard boys. He blamed himself for the pummeling. He said he'd thought that Harvard boys were all talk and he hadn't even lifted his hands. Wayne laughs and nods.

After the tests and the MRI, the neurologist wrote in her assessment that Brian seemed shocked when he got the diagnosis. I tell Wayne, I don't think he was shocked. I think it was terrible to have his worst fears confirmed and he was seeking to understand all the implications as quickly as possible. I say, He didn't want to be caught flat-footed, like he was by those Harvard boys.

Great Wayne listens, not looking at me. He tells me about his experiences with the draft during the Vietnam War (he was drafted as a doctor, and he served. He says they told him he could serve as a doctor or as an infantryman but that he'd be serving, either way). He says he did everything he could to help young men looking for deferments, in and out of the Army. (I think this is what he said. I was gripping the arms of the chair so tightly, my hands hurt, and because my heart was beating in my ears, I couldn't keep up with his sentences.) After some time, he says, So, yes, I can help you with this.

I bend over in the chair, covering my face, and cry. Wayne sits there quietly, like he's supposed to. When I lift my head, Wayne says that I should call for an appointment for Brian, that it will be about ninety minutes and he'll write up his findings, whatever they are, and if the findings are helpful to our cause, we can then send his letter to Dignitas. He suggests that I might want to be at the interview. Why? I say. Do you need me to be there? Wayne shrugs (an elaborate, shrinky shrug, the kind that means: I have a very good reason, which I will not tell you) and says, Well, you might be glad afterward that you'd been present.

I am, in fact, very glad that I was present. It was a master class in interviewing. I could see all of Brian's cognitive gaps as if someone had shone a flashlight on the cave wall. I watched Wayne help Brian go forward and backward in time, with tenderness and attention, taking him through very specific exercises and a wide-ranging conversation, and I also got to watch my husband enjoying one last warm, in-depth chat with another Yale man who knew football.

These are the final paragraphs of Wayne's letter about Brian, and this letter is what gets us the green light from Dignitas.

> I found no evidence in Mr. Ameche's history or presentation of *clinical* depression. No profound mood disturbances with weight loss, difficulty sleeping, or lost time from work. In reviewing his past experience, I think that he was over-diagnosed by himself and those who had treated him years ago. It seems more appropriate to say

that what he complained of was a situational dysphoria
brought on by expectable life stressors, challenges, and
disappointments. It seems likely that his adult distress
had its roots in the dysfunctional family setting of his
childhood. He is the oldest of six children of a legend-
ary American football hero and his loving but limited
wife. He himself was an outstanding football player at
Yale University, where he also began his architectural
studies. He married his teenage childhood sweetheart.
This was a union that did not stand the test of matu-
rity that comes with adult life. They divorced without
children. The divorce caused upheaval in Mr. Ameche's
devout Italian-American Catholic family of origin.
For the past 12 years he has been in a stable, satisfying,
and replenishing marriage that has brought with it his
wife Amy's children and grandchildren. As he reported
movingly, he has found great love, joy, and meaning,
surrounded by them.

   Mr. Ameche estimates that he has 60–80 percent of
his recent memory capacity left. I would estimate that it
is at more like 40–50 percent. When asked for his social
security number at a relaxed moment, he provided it
haltingly. He could not repeat it backwards. His memory functioning comes and goes, both within the session
and day to day. He is probably made more aware of the
perplexity and frustration that are set off by those lapses
from the reactions of those around him. He delivers his
narrative in plain, straightforward, yet poignant terms.
Some aspects of his presentation seem quite common-
place. He and his wife derive pleasure from the rhythm

of ordinary everyday activities such as running errands
and shopping for home goods. He has led a fulfilling
physical life, close to nature; fishing and building (retirement complexes, athletic facilities, etc.). He abhors a
compromised existence lit only by a flickering, fading
cognitive flame as he submerges into the darkness of
an expiring existence and death, after the fact. At the
moment he is mentally competent with sound judgment
that is unhampered by mental illness or severe character disorder. In the midst of his current affliction he falls
within the range of normal when it comes to charting
his life's course and making decisions.

He is a strong, determined man of mettle and cour-
age.

Great Wayne sent the letter to me within a week. I emailed
him back, thanking him and asking him to throw around any
titles he had or ever had had. He laid the titles on, until the
list looked like a parody of a psychoanalytic Who's Who, and
if he had been that kind of guy, he would have added *Rufus T.
Firefly, Prime Minister of Freedonia*. I send the letter to Dignitas
and I wait to hear from Heidi. I don't think I should show the
letter to Brian and he doesn't ask to see it.

"I enjoyed talking with Wayne," he says. "The man knows
all about Fordham's Seven Blocks of Granite offensive line.
Good man."

End of November 2019, Stony Creek

It's the day before Thanksgiving and Brian has had one more Dignitas phone interview (he remembers the word *Alzheimer's;* he remembers that it's Switzerland, not Sweden), and Heidi tells us we now have the provisional green light. She reveals that her name is really S. We thank her quietly. S. sighs, like a pilot who has safely landed the plane. She says, Mr. Ameche, please have a nice weekend. Mrs. Bloom, you, too. She tells us that there will be more emails coming with more details and more documents needed. This is the call we have been working toward since August.

We've heard what we needed to hear, and in the first moment, Brian hugs me hard, because we have accomplished the thing we wanted to accomplish, and done it together, and he loves teamwork. And then the light changes and dims; I am in the world without him in it; he sees, clearly, the world going on without him, me alone in the kitchen and him not next to me. After we make sure we've hung up properly, we cry in each other's arms and, without speaking, we go right up to bed for a nap, at 11 A.M., and only come down when the kids come through the door, ready to start Thanksgiving prep.

I tell the kids, while Brian makes a sandwich, in his usual fussy, happily attentive way. We are all crammed in the kitchen, relieved, in an awful way, relieved that Brian will be able to do what he wishes to do, and, except for Brian, we are weepy and distressed. Brian takes my daughter Caitlin aside and tells her that she must take care of me, and she promises that she will, and I cry in the doorway. He finishes his sandwich and goes upstairs, to watch the news.

I start dropping things. I drop the ceramic pie weights onto the kitchen floor. I drop an entire open bottle of corn syrup into a bowl of butter and eggs. I burn the toast. I actually set one pie on fire in the oven and quadruple the amount of bourbon in the other so that no one who is not a Kentucky drunk could eat it. It's not just that I can't hold on to anything (metaphor received) but how little I care and how little effort I'm prepared to make to fix any of it. I gather up most of the pie weights and just tell everyone to be careful where they walk. The mothers of the grandchildren hunt down every pie weight I missed, and I let them. I throw out the bottle of corn syrup and then I throw out the butter and eggs, too. I leave the burnt toast in the toaster oven and figure that someone, at some point, will need to use the toaster oven and they will remove the blackened toast. I think, And this is how you get to Grey Gardens.

I don't have the energy to run around in a leotard and

anklets, but I see how old people get used to dust and stickiness, mild filth and mildewed towels. It's not because they are too blind or weak to do anything about these problems necessarily but because they have just seen too much. When you've buried all your closest friends, how worked up can you get about a trace of lipstick on a coffee cup or a ribbon of dust on the frame of the photo of someone you'll never see again? You've buried two wives and two brothers who loved you and left you—how seriously can you take the worn spot (now sort of a hole) at the back of the chair? Perspective is useful, of course: It's why very few people want to be eighteen again. But the other side is having so much perspective, it's hard to give a damn about anything happening here in the real.

Children are always the exception for me, and I am watching them all, my three and their four, and I'm grateful because if not for them, we'd be living in filth already, remote in hand.

Thanksgiving is done, Christmas is coming, and so is my mother-in-law.

Brian and I already knew the broad outlines, and the details, of Alzheimer's from the story of my mother-in-law's best friend of fifty years. Yvonne's best friend was an aunt to Brian, a regular dinner guest, formidably well dressed in the Nancy Reagan mold (the custom pantsuit with the matching navy-and-white silk flower on the lapel and the sapphire earrings to match; I admired her), a great golfer, a devoted philanthropist (to causes I reviled), and my mother-in-law's boon companion for movies, dinner, and drinks at the club. She had descended into Alzheimer's these last few years, as if on an express. First she complained about the cleaning lady, then she complained about her occasional guests, then she complained about her son. Then she complained that valuables were being moved to odd places and probably stolen. Then she could no longer navigate, not even during the day, not even on roads she'd driven for fifty years, and my mother-in-law had to drive them to the club and to the late-afternoon movies. Then she became violent and tearful, afraid of the terrible real and imaginary forces beyond her control. Then her son placed her in an assisted-living facility, which she resented and complained about loudly, and then she didn't have the capacity to behave well in the communal dining room or dress appropriately for the yoga class or even to keep herself clean and get along with her healthcare aide. Then her son moved her into a memory-care unit. And then she lost a tooth, and then another, and sat on her bed, waiting to leave. She was clean enough but badly dressed and she still knew my mother-in-law and, weeping at every visit, begged her friend to take her home. My mother-in-law had not spared us the details.

In early December, Yvonne arrives for a visit. We have some kind of dinner, all wonderful Italian food brought by Yvonne, and Yvonne has a splash of vodka and we go to bed early. Yvonne and I are up very early. (I think I saw the sunrise every day that year.) Brian and I decide it's time to share our loose plan with her—that right before we took off for Zurich, Brian would send his family an email letting them know of his decision to go to Dignitas, and afterward I would send everyone, friends and family, a second letter, shaped by him, about his death:

Dear Friends,

Some of you know, and some of you do not: Brian was diagnosed with early-onset Alzheimer's this past summer. It has been a difficult, demanding, and heartbreaking time and through it all, two things have been unwavering: our loving and supportive families and Brian's considered and clear decision that he would not and did not choose "the long goodbye" of Alzheimer's, over the next ten years.

Brian, who loved his lucky wife, his life, and all of the fishing, football, fiction, and family it contained, made arrangements to end his life, peacefully and painlessly, at Dignitas in Zurich, with me by his side.

He was, throughout this time, remarkably courageous while grief-stricken and warm, loving, and engaged with all of us, even as he faced the end of his life. He continued with art, with walks on the Trolley Trail of Stony Creek, and with his service to Planned Parenthood, to which he was deeply committed.

The memorial service for Brian Ameche will be at 3:00 on Saturday, February 8, 2020, at the Willoughby Wallace Library, Branford, Connecticut. We would be very glad to see you there. (If you have any questions about the service, please contact: XXX at XXX@gmail.com.)

If you wish to commemorate his life, please make a donation to Planned Parenthood.

Love to you all,
Amy

Brian plans to send his email just before we get on the plane. That way, there'll be no chance of any of them interfering, he said; I'll have said goodbye to each of them, even if they don't know it.

It wasn't a great plan and eventually we improved it. It didn't give his siblings much room and it didn't give us much time for the truly final farewells, but as far as Brian was concerned, they'd be informed with no room to interfere, and that was what mattered to him.

I hadn't said anything to Yvonne over the phone but couldn't keep my mouth shut with her in person and in our house, my unlikely champion and a woman who had four children under the age of five by the time she was twenty-five and was now going to lose her beautiful boy, having already suffered the death of Brian's youngest brother, Paul (the sweetest one of us, Brian said). I loved my mother-in-law, and even though Brian had made a decision to leave the family circle of Philadelphia, he loved her, too, respected the hell out of her resilience and determination and often quoted a favorite saying of hers: We're not here for a long time, we're here for a good time.

You can imagine how often he said that.

(As I was arriving to meet Yvonne for the first time, Brian, not even divorced from his first wife, decided to give his mother all the bad news at once, an hour before I showed up: three kids, divorced, career, Jewish, and bisexual. She didn't bat an eye. After our first dinner together, she patted my hand and went to the kitchen to call his siblings and basically said, Get on board with this.)

. . .

Even so, Yvonne, very Catholic, always neatly coiffed, given to wearing a nice Burberry wrap over her St. John suit and not much given to exploring worlds that were truly foreign to her, is not my ideal confidante. I stand outside Yvonne's bedroom door on our second floor until I hear footsteps and wait until I hear bustling sounds. I knock and she lets me in; she's already nicely put together. I sit on the bed, beside her, and tell her our plan with Dignitas. She pulls away from me and wipes her eyes and I wait, with my hands clasped. I don't want a scene, but if there is one, I want it to happen while Brian is still asleep.

Then she says, "I am so relieved. I realized that last night. I was praying about this and praying all night and I realized that what I prayed for was that he would not have to suffer as Joanne does. I'm shocked that I'm so relieved, but I am."

Yvonne talks about the tragic life and the terrible death to come of her dear, glamorous, devoted friend. We hold hands and cry and she says that I was a gift to her son and I throw myself in her arms, as if she is my own mother. We go downstairs to have breakfast with Brian. Yvonne holds Brian's hand and talks about Buddy, a quadriplegic young man whom she knew well. Over coffee, she tells us how Buddy's brother drove him to a motel (in Michigan? This must be what it's like for Brian on bad days: Whose brother? When was this? Do I have to listen?). There they'd arranged to meet with Jack Kevorkian (the Dr. Death of the Eighties), who gave Buddy a lethal injection.

Brian says, Well, this whole thing, it's in your sweet spot, Mom. He means death and dying. Yvonne nods agreeably. I go upstairs and come down to model which of two scarves I should wear for my lunch with my new agent. I wear the one Yvonne chooses: Sophisticated, not somber, she says. I have no idea how I look these days, and Brian, who used to have things to say (usually nice things), doesn't notice. For years I asked his opinion about what I wore, and for the last three years I fussed at him about his clothes—fishing hat plus Brooks Brothers polo = homeless—and now I don't do either.

We ask Yvonne not to tell Brian's siblings about our plans. She doesn't hesitate.

"It's not mine to tell," she says. "It's your business. You tell them when you're ready."

"I know it's a hard secret to keep," I say.

In the most ladylike way, she snorts. "I'm eighty-four," she says. "I can keep a secret."

Brian smiles and says to his mother—again—that she's an expert in death. Yvonne cared for and buried her barely middle-aged parents when she was young; a beloved younger sister, for whom Yvonne's home became a hospice; an equally beloved older sister; her sweet son, Paul, still at college; and two much-loved husbands. I am leaving out—as Yvonne would point out—all of her late friends.

She says that she's been to eight funerals in the last six months, and she lists each of her friends and their circum-stances of death and family. (Stroke, husband has ALS. Heart, kids are in Los Angeles. Like that.) She's sadly matter-of-fact.

She cheers herself up by recalling the film her family made (*A Family in Grief: The Ameche Story*) after Paul's death, as part of a projected series of documentaries on resiliency; their particular film was on the rest of the family in the aftermath of Paul's car accident on Christmas Eve in 1981. Yvonne says she remembers Brian saying, in his voice-over narration, that death is something we don't talk about but that there is no life without death. I can see that she and Brian are both quite pleased that he was so wise at such a young age.

I'm a crabby, exhausted person, ready for a nap at any and every hour of the day. I pour myself a third cup of coffee and think, Duh—and the man was close to thirty when he made that remark. There is going to be some Ameche myth-making coming about Brian's prescient sensitivity and Dalai Lama–ness. Everything makes me mad. Yvonne loves her children and casts each of them in the most flattering baby-pink spotlight whenever she can, and I tend to resist, for no good reason. I'm the grumpy usher at the show muttering about spaghetti stains on the satin and flubbed lines. Then, as now, I don't quite understand how this film project developed, but the film about the Ameches did air and I do know that my mother-in-law had and enjoyed a brief career speaking about grief at various conferences, following the making of the film. What Yvonne manages to do, in the days after Brian's diagnosis and in the days after Brian's death, is to locate herself exactly where all the guide-to-grief people say she should be. At home, by herself, with her daughters or with friends, she lets herself be a mother awash in grief. We have one brief phone call in which she weeps to me that she just wanted more of him, and I feel so much the same way that instead of comforting her, as I intended, I just weep with her and then we mumble our goodbyes into our wet phones.

With us, and then later with me, she doesn't center her grief. She's careful not to cry first or loudest and she rarely refers to her own loss. She is, as Brian says, a fucking class act.

On the way to the train station with Yvonne and Brian, I concentrate on my driving. (During this year, I will have five car accidents, one totaling my car. At least four of these are entirely my fault.) I overhear pieces of a lively conversation about whether or not Father Bob, whom I gather Yvonne has in mind for Brian's Philadelphia memorial service, which I didn't know was being planned, is gay. There's some back-and-forth, but in the end they both shrug, express their affection, hers great, his mild, for Father Bob, and Brian tells his mother that if she wants to have a service for him in a Philadelphia church, he doesn't mind. He also says that he might like his ashes buried with his father and Paul, and my first thought is that he has now planned for four different resting places for his ashes. Yvonne is pleased with all aspects of this and then she is gone, the first of the parade of Ameches to our house.

While we were battling to work things out with Dignitas, we were vague with his family about what would happen next, and even vaguer about our hopes for what would happen next. One of his brothers said something like, One day at a time, and we mm-hmm'ed. The same brother said that *another* brother had noticed something was wrong with Brian the last time Brian had come home, in the spring, before the diagnosis. That spring, as Yvonne was emptying out her house to move into an assisted-living apartment, she instructed her five adult children to come get the things she didn't want. She told Brian that the giant (three-hundred-sixty-pound) stuffed shark he'd caught when he was sixteen was waiting for him, in her basement. He wanted it. Reader, I did not. I wanted him to have what he wanted, most of the time, but not this shark on the short walls of our small house.

I suggested Yale might want the fish (I would have offered it to his elementary school, to our library, to Lenny & Joe's Fish Tale restaurant, up the road. Anywhere but our house), and after I had made some phone calls and determined that none of the colleges wanted a giant stuffed shark with a few missing teeth, we moved on to the Yale Fishing Club (yes, they exist, and now I love them) and their particular arena, the Yale Outdoor Education Center. Getting the shark meant driving two hundred miles to his mother's house and back, in a U-Haul rental truck, then driving thirty-five miles on to the Yale Outdoor Etc., unloading the shark, doing the handoff with Mr. Yale Outdoor Etc., and coming home, in one day.

Brian and I worked on this project, him identifying the who and what and me either making the calls or making the on-paper guidance for the calls. (What time do they open? What time do they close? Can someone help you load/unload the shark?) We were like those shambling old couples at the beach—he looks for the shells and she picks them up, clutching each other for balance. It took two weeks, but all was arranged and Brian managed it, calling me hourly and coming home safely, exhausted but calm. The only glitch, apparently, was an angry misunderstanding with one of his brothers. This brother is a stickler for routine and cannot bear to be wrong, so I didn't think anything of it. I didn't even really take notice of how hard this all was to arrange, how many phone calls to the same people, how many more follow-up calls than usual. We just did it.

I'm glad he got the shark before the diagnosis, before we knew that he shouldn't be driving. By the end of the summer, when Mr. Yale Outdoor Etc. called Brian a few times asking for the details for the shark's plaque, for its magnificent display, it was impossible for Brian to keep track of the task or the details. He had forgotten exactly where he caught it and the circumstances, although we have a (large, gold-framed) photo of him at sixteen, long blond hair and tube socks, standing with his father on his one side and the shark on the other.

Later, after we share Brian's diagnosis, all of his siblings will tell me that they knew something was wrong on the Shark Trip, and I am angry but not surprised that not one of them called me to say, Is Brian okay? I don't know why it makes me angry. I don't know if it's the thought of them seeing and discussing his vulnerability or that they didn't hasten to share their observations with me and offer support. (Would I want them to? Would I want one of his sisters calling up to say, Hoo boy, Brian is definitely getting absentminded. Who would that help?) I am just angry that they saw him struggle and they got to do that and he is gone and they are here. Mostly, when I am angry, it is only that.

The sun sets at 4:28 P.M. and we are still working out a few kinks with Dignitas. (It takes Brian less than five minutes to find a copy of his birth certificate, which astounds and delights us both. We scan it and send it. I scan it and send it.) Dignitas writes back the next day that, although we are on course, they do need the certificate itself. We send it. Two weeks later, I hear from S. that it was not *quite* the form they need. We contact Kenosha Birth Records and, ten days later, we receive the new certificate. We send the actual certificate to Dignitas. Ten days after that, they email us that this new form is acceptable and we are even more firmly green-lit.

We finally give Yvonne the okay to share the plan with the siblings. I say that we are available for all supportive conversations and for visits. When a sister-in-law strongly suggests that we have a big family dinner in Philly as a way to celebrate Brian and say goodbye, I say no, in four different and emphatic ways, and I know the visits will be coming. And I'm mostly glad. I'm not going to Philadelphia again, Brian says.

His sisters call me, as well as Brian. They are loving and distraught. One will come for a visit in a week, with Yvonne. The other will come with her husband, of whom Brian is very fond. One brother will make yet another trip with Yvonne. His other brother is, I think, supposed to come with a sister-in-law. Brian's niece has volunteered to keep track of the schedule, and she does her best but, in the end, she calls me and lets me know that, as I anticipated, the coordination of visits kind of broke down and people are doing as they damn well will. I appreciate her more than I can say, this lovely, anxious girl who *volunteered* to wrangle her aunts and uncles and grand-mother into a schedule of coordinated visits to say a final fare-well to Brian. I wouldn't have wanted the job and she has helped more than she hasn't, having conveyed to her family that Brian's convenience and comfort are paramount, that Amy is a Rottweiler and will not have it any other way.

In the end, one sister-in-law and one brother-in-law, not married to each other (whom I have never known to be close), decide to come up together, which surprises all of us, even Brian, and then there is some friction about scheduling, or driving, or avoiding rush hour, and he will not make the trip with her but he is not pleased that she'll make the trip without him. He will come a week later, with Yvonne. Meanwhile, our sister-in-law does make the trip by herself. She arrives with food and kisses, and I can see Brian is truly happy to see her, with her pretty face and warm hugs and her admiration for him. She could stay for a week, as far as I'm concerned. She is a lively, mile-a-minute presence and we're glad of it and glad she came, despite the family-wide disapproval of her coming up solo. (I'm not sure why that was. If they were my own family, I could tell you why, even if I chose not to. Brian's family is still, to me, another country, where I speak the language but not the dialect.) The family phone calls with Brian seem to go well. There are a few lovely letters from friends of Yvonne's, who've known him since he was born. He becomes more detached with every week.

We get several emails from an old friend, imploring and scolding and using, again and again, the least compelling arguments I can imagine (I read on Google . . . There's no urgency . . .), and each time Brian responds with kindness and restraint.

Nothing will happen until January. There's Christmas and Hanukkah to get through before January 6, when Dignitas reopens. No one is happy about this, except, maybe, in the oddest way: me. I know that this will be our last Christmas, but I know that we will still have some time after that.

I tell my sister that Brian and I won't be joining her and her husband for the posh Vermont resort New Year's Eve that we've done with them for the last few years. Ellen wants me to come. She says, Maybe it would be a nice distraction. She says, I just want us to go on having what we had. This is loving and heartfelt, but I can feel my own heart harden. That will never happen again in my life, I think, and I say, as harshly as I can, that neither he nor I will be sitting around—not even over tins of caviar and French champagne—chitchatting with people whose favorite conversation is: We are planning a fabulous trip in the spring, and what great trips are you planning? That'll be awkward. I say it unkindly and my sister, who loves me, says, Got it.

I can hardly stand to talk to my sister on Christmas Day; it's the first time we've been apart for Jewish Christmas (Chinese food on Christmas Eve, glass dreidels and fortune cookies on the tree) in more than thirty years. When it's over, Brian goes upstairs to nurse his cold and I start untrimming the tree.

I am practicing being a widow, preparing myself to do things alone: taking down the strings of lights by myself, listening to Brittany Howard, and having a snack. It is about as much like actual widowhood as our granddaughter Ivy making a fist and waving it overhead, saying ferociously: "When I do like this, I am *magic,* and you cannot catch me." When we are being perfect grandparents, we pretend we can't catch her. Sometimes, in the spirit of my own grandfather, I am a darkly cheerful beacon of realism and I just go ahead and catch her.

I'm waiting in the living room, pretending and knowing that I will be caught and that I am not a widow, I'm just a weeping and annoyed wife. Brian will be gone from my life soon, although I don't yet know how soon, and he's also still a man with a cold. It's a cold, not pleurisy, is what I think, even as I am tearing the fringe off a pillow at the thought of his not being upstairs any longer, not having a cold, not being a sick man than whom there is no one sicker, as I have said to him. One time, I said that I had friends with metastatic breast cancer who complained less about that than he did about his cold. And then he won't be there for me to say it to him.

. . .

I had two big relationships before Brian, and both ended because I wanted out. I didn't feel truly lonely in either one until toward the end, because I had my kids and my friends and my work and a great deal of pleasure in solitude. Even when I felt ignored or put upon or mildly mistreated, I knew that the other person loved me and needed me, and even if they were not who I had hoped they'd be, I knew that I was big in their lives. Sometimes now with Brian, I am worse than alone. I'm gone from his interior landscape. Not that I have been uprooted but that I am not there, and never was. These moments are scorching. Instead of yelling at Brian, Hey, I'm a person, too, I make him a cup of tea with a big spoonful of honey and bring it upstairs. He opens his eyes and smiles and he says, Thank you, and I get to see that it's just as scorching to be present.

I call Susie Chang for a Tarot reading, since she and Great Wayne are now the only professionals I turn to, and I tell her that Dignitas has us on hold until January 6. I ask her what she sees for this trip. It's my only question. She tells me she's getting out the traditional Rider-Waite deck, which is to me the "let's get down to business" deck. No distracting beauty, no metaphorical crows, no modern re-gendering. (I have opinions about these things. The summer I was seventeen, my Friday-night job was to shill for Madame Rosa, next to San-dolino's, in the Village. My job was to walk up and down in front of her storefront, handing out flyers and saying things like: Madame Rosa, five bucks, knows all. Before Madame

Rosa closed for the night, before I got on the train back to Long Island, I'd make her a cup of tea and we'd chat briefly. "Look at the shoes," she said. "As a rule, rich people don't wear cheap shoes." "Look at the hands, soft or hard." "No one comes here because they're happy, kiddo." She was as good a clinical supervisor as I ever had. Madame Rosa used a Rider-Waite deck, and she told me that she had one of the originals, made in 1910.)

Susie Chang says that it will go well, no real hitches. I ask her if they'll change their minds, once we are in Zurich. (In my mind, these are serious psychiatric examinations by serious physicians. Even though S. has now shared her actual name with us, she has continued to stress the "provisional" in "pro-visional green light," in every conversation.) Susie Chang pulls the card for Brian and it is a man crossing a bridge. He will be fine, she says; he is determined to go forward and the bridge holds. I keep crying. She stops talking. I tell her that they will probably offer us a choice of dates.

"You must take the first date they give you," she says.

"Well," I say. "That might mean we have to get ready in a—"

"You need to take the first date they give you. I'm not saying you can't overcome the difficulties that will arise if you take a later date, but I do see difficulties." (As it turns out, by the time I fly home, the first reports of COVID are beginning.)

My Husband

When I met Brian (well, not exactly when I met him; when I met him I thought he was arrogant, tedious about fishing, and needing a haircut), he reminded me just a little of someone. It wasn't my mother and it wasn't my father, a man who had excellent DNA and the romance and joie de vivre of a doorstop. I already knew that the Virtuous—people who cannot face their own flaws or acknowledge the ugliness in their nature, people who will patiently explain, for *days*, that you should not be hurt by their behavior because they didn't mean to hurt you—those people are not for me. Brian, as it turned out, was at peace with all his faults (even the serious ones), and most of the time, I loved him for that, too.

Before the diagnosis, Brian made jokes about taking up drinking again. I was never a good audience. When we were dating, Brian drank a large double vodka most nights. He was

stunned when I told him that the standard measurement for a
vodka on the rocks was just a two-ounce pour (thank you for
the training, Red's Bar and Grille and also Valentino's Café).
My children, who had lived through plenty of genteel alco-
hol abuse already, in my previous relationships, were horrified to come home for a visit and find a handle of vodka in
my freezer. (I drink—but like a Jew, and not like one of my
schnapps-slamming ancestors, either.)

I come from a family where there was a bottle of Tío
Pepe in the sideboard, gathering dust for years. Once, at my
parents' house, when I made myself a second gin and tonic,
my mother worried aloud about what was happening to me
up there in Connecticut. I didn't ask Brian to stop, but I did
ask him not to drink at my professional occasions. At one big
literary festival, I'd been bored and annoyed and made the
mistake of telling Brian so. Ten minutes later, fueled by alco-
hol, his general undauntedness released, he'd paid one of the
shuttle drivers, scheduled to start driving the speakers back
to the hotel in a few hours, to bring the two of us back to our
hotel right then. I had to explain myself to the nice driver, let
him keep the fifty dollars, and tell Brian that I could not and
should not leave so early. Brian napped in the minibus until I
felt it was respectable to leave. He didn't drink at my professional events after that or at our wedding, and six weeks later,
he stopped drinking altogether, forever.

In the last few years, Brian would say, Can I start drinking
again when I'm eighty? And I'd say, Please, don't ever start
drinking again, but you can start smoking weed when you're
eighty (he was aggressive when drunk and a cuddly chatterbox
when high), and then he'd say, reasonably, that he wouldn't get

high *or* have a drink until he was eighty-five and I would agree that eighty-five was fine but if he got drunk and fell down, even at ninety, I wasn't going to help him up and he would say, Fair.

I married him—despite all the very good reasons that no one should ever partner up for a third time—because early on, he reminded me of the best father figure of my life, my ninth-grade English teacher. When that man died, his friends (eighty-year-old poker buddies, pals from his teaching days, devoted former students of all ages and types) wept. He was old, fat, diabetic, and often brusque. Women desired him and my children loved him and most men liked his company a great deal. He was loyal, imperious, needy, charming, big-hearted, and just about the most selfish, lovable, and foolishly fearless person I had ever known. And then I met Brian and found another.

On our third anniversary, Brian hurt his back. I'd come home to find him in our bedroom, not dressed, more than naked. He'd left work early. He was wearing his T-shirt, a very wide, white, and necessary mesh-and-Velcro lumbar-support wrap, and the navy-blue socks that were usually hidden by his suit trousers. His boxers were off because he was going to bed; his undershirt and socks were on because his terrible back pain made both the reaching up and the bending over difficult. He looked at himself in the mirror and laughed out loud. He put his black fedora on his head and modeled the whole look for me, like Naomi Campbell. That's what it was like.

The night passes and the next morning we have a car take us to Pfaffikon, where Dignitas has its apartment, or house—I couldn't really tell. It's a residential structure in an industrial park. Two nice women, in nice clothes, sweaters and slacks (I mean that I feel an effort was made. They didn't just throw on their sweats and come over), greet us. They have dressed for the occasion of shepherding us across the river and they take it seriously. I have never been treated with such seamless, attentive tact. They walk us in, up a few steps to the door, and I see a snow-covered garden, the kind of gesture toward a garden that you'd find in an industrial park (it's January, so it might be that it's a floral paradise in June), and into a large, odd, immaculate room. There's seating in every corner—two small armchairs, a large pleather recliner, a pleather sofa, and a hospital bed, as well. It dawns on me

later that it's important that everything that can be sat on or
laid down upon be washable. In the center of the room there's
a table with several chairs. The Ladies bring our paperwork
to the table and point out the many bowls of chocolates. They
review all of the steps, which Brian and I can now both recite.
They look at him closely and say, At any time in this process,
including after you drink the anti-emetic, you can choose not
to do this. We will be very supportive of you changing your
mind, rest assured. We are assured. The only sign of reluc-
tance on Brian's part is what he warned me about—his making conversation before taking the sodium pentobarbital.
He'd said to me that he thought he might be inclined to "just
bullshit around for a while" when the time came to take it. "I
know I have to go," he said. "I know I'm going. I'm ready. I'm
just not going to hurry."

He doesn't hurry. He drinks the anti-emetic and gets comfortable on the couch. I sit next to him, holding his hand, but
I have to let it go because he's gesturing while storytelling.
The stories are all about football at Yale and his coach, Carm
Cozza, and I could tell them with him: Brian and a friend
winding up in jail because of a young, dumb fight in front of
the Anchor Bar, and Carm Cozza, stern and forgiving, bail-
ing them out; Brian talking about quitting football because
he didn't get to play enough his first season and Carm telling him that he, Carm, would let Brian play when Brian was
good enough and not before and Brian resolving to be good
enough; Brian's father and Carm Cozza playing handball
together one time, his two fathers.

I cannot manage to look interested in these stories, because
I'm not (Brian says nothing about his life, about our life, about

our love, about the children and grandchildren, nothing about the beautiful public housing he designed and cared about so deeply or the work he did for conservation and open spaces or even, and you know I must be reaching here, about fishing), but I do try not to look like I'm in agony, which I am.

The Ladies wait in the back room (a kitchen, I think), and after about forty-five minutes they come out again. They tell us that the anti-emetic has now worn off and if Brian wishes to continue (I do, he says), he will have to take it again. They say, You can take your time, and I roll my eyes because of course he will, he always does, I think, as if we are in some other room, on some other occasion, and then I remember where I am and I'm ashamed of myself. Brian smiles slightly. "What time's your plane?" he says, and I have never felt so bad about being me in my entire life.

He takes the anti-emetic again and the Ladies put an airplane pillow around his neck. Brian falls silent and now I long for the football stories. I take both of his hands and he lets me. IloveyouIloveyouIloveyou, I say. I love you so much. I love you, too, he says, and he drinks the sodium pentobarbital. I kiss him, all over his handsome, weary face, and he lets me.

It is impossible to think about the next twenty minutes. I keep my eyes and hands on him, as if I'll forget what it is like to breathe next to him or feel his presence. (I don't, not for a minute. I hear his breathing when I go to sleep and I feel his body heat when I wake up.) He falls asleep holding my hand and his head falls back a little on the neck pillow (whose purpose I now understand). His breathing changes and it's the last time I will hear him sleeping, breathing deeply and steadily, the way he has done lying beside me for almost fifteen years. I hold his hand. I can still feel its weight and warmth. His skin color changes, from ruddy to paler pink. I sit there and sit there, as if some other thing will now happen. He is quite pale and I see that he is gone from this world.

I sit, holding his hand, for a long time. I get up and wrap my arms around him and kiss his forehead, as if he is my baby, at last gone to sleep, as if he is my brave boy going on a long journey, miles and miles of Nought.

The Temple Gatekeepers

The Ladies emerge from the kitchen at some point and they sit by, quiet and prepared, the temple gatekeepers. Although I have tried to think about this before, I have no idea what to do with Brian's things: his coat, his muffler, his suitcase and the clothes in it, his medications. The Ladies offer that they can take care of all of that and his clothes will be given to people who need them.

There's not much else to do. The Ladies would like me to go, before the Swiss police come. It is simpler, they say. It doesn't feel that we have done something illegal, but I can tell that it would be better (perhaps better for me? For Dignitas?) for me to not be around while a Swiss policeman identifies Brian's body (that's what his passport and dental records are for, as I understand it). I call an Uber and hug the Ladies. I head to the airport.

· · ·

In Zurich Airport, I sit in the fancy lounge and I look around for faces, people-watching. It is very pleasant in the Swissair lounge coming home. I'm wearing Brian's wedding ring on my right hand, on my forefinger, and it's much too big. I gesture once, while talking to my friend, and the ring flies off, nearly hitting a man in the face. It rolls under a chair and I get it and sit in that chair, staring out the window, avoiding men's faces. Since the moment of Brian's death, I find most people, especially men, disgusting. Not just unappealing but disgusting—like yesterday's oatmeal. Like eels in a bowl. I find heterosexual couples dismaying. In the lounge, I feel like an alien examining pairs of earthlings: What is the meaning of that? How could a creature like that be the choice this other creature makes? How can one recognize choice in these random movements?

The men without women upset me more: There's a lanky, dark-skinned man across from me, chewing cheese and crackers with his mouth open. The cheddar and the pumpernickel crisps are distinct. The old white man two seats away from me is digging into a bowl of gnocchi with tomato sauce. His tie and his whole face are freckled with sauce. I see a man on my other side, a few armchairs away. Very big, very black. Thanks to Brian, I now divide men into football/not football. This man is very wide and very tall. A running refrigerator, Brian would have said. He has a nice smile and I immediately think that I would be squirming out from under him after a pleasant evening and calling 911. Most men disgust me, and even the mildest feeling of attraction apparently leads directly to imagining them dead and cooling beside me.

I've internalized Great Wayne, so I hear him saying: You haven't even metabolized Brian's absence, let alone his death, yet.

I tell Wayne that right now I'm imagining a lovely, interested, interesting person across from me in a nice restaurant, and then I'm so nauseous in real life, I get out of my chair to run to the ladies' room.

When I come back, Internalized Wayne is waiting for me. He shakes his head.

You can stop making an effort, he says.

I almost stop. I call everyone who must be called: my children, Brian's mother, Brian's two sisters. I text one of Brian's brothers. His other brother barely uses a computer and doesn't text. I ask the brother I do reach, M., to get hold of the other brother and tell him that Brian died peacefully and painlessly and I am now on the way home. I say the same thing to everyone. Brian's sisters and their husbands (I don't remember who's in the group sitting with my mother-in-law, I remember only that there is a group sitting together, praying and waiting and, I hope, being of great comfort to one another) have been gathered together at Yvonne's apartment. As I keep texting and dialing and scrolling, I think most of her, who has been such a rock and a support and a surprise through all of this. I play with Brian's ring until our flight is called.

Thursday Evening, January 30, 2020, Leaving Zurich

My daughter Sarah waits for me at Newark Airport, my son, Alex, texts us along the way, and my daughter Caitlin waits up for Sarah and me at my house in Stony Creek. They help me upstairs, to my bedroom on the third floor, because I am moving like a blind, drunk stranger. Every light downstairs is ablaze, as I like it, as is my bad habit. When we get to my bedroom, Caitlin goes to turn on the overhead light. There is a snap and a fizz and then nothing. We flip the other switches. We try to turn on the bedside lamps. Light comes on in the bathroom and in the closet but none in the bedroom. Joe the Gentleman Electrician comes the next day. He changes every lightbulb and fools with the circuit breaker in the basement and comes back into the house and still nothing. He sighs. Suddenly, the lights come on. He's as baffled as I am. It's Brian being playful, we say. In the course of the next few days, every appliance in my house will break down and need to be repaired or replaced. I had thought, or hoped, that I would curl up in a despairing heap in the middle of my bed for two weeks and crawl out only for tea. Wayne asks me, Have you ever, at the worst time in your life, taken to your bed like that? I say that this *is* the worst time in my life and no. But I always wanted to, I say.

Instead of lying in bed wanly, I get up the next day and make coffee and am glad to be in my own house. I have put aside Brian's cuff links and watches for my children, and the notes to them from Brian, and, in a small box, the notes he wrote to the granddaughters. The girls and I give a lot of Brian's clothes to Goodwill, because his clothes are too big for anyone else in the family. I save everything I cannot bear to give away, including his Yale golf jacket, which is an awful thing, and his undershirts, which all the granddaughters wear as night-gowns. I put all the condolence notes in a big bowl and I put my thank-you stationery in another bowl and I put both bowls in the back of his side of the closet. I send Caitlin and Sarah back to their families.

I eat oddly but not badly. I think about getting drunk but don't. I wake up at 5 A.M. and by now seeing the sunrise is a habit and 6:15 means I can legitimately get up and make more coffee. I watch television, and I will have seen every episode of *Brooklyn Nine-Nine*. I sit in my office and look at the pale-blue sky and the cold water. I listen to music all day, every-thing except Bill Evans and Billie Holiday, because I just can't take it. I plan the memorial service. Right before we went to

Zurich, Brian had finally stopped reading *As I Lay Dying*, after weeks of jotting down the names of all the characters, so he could keep track. (I don't think you have to have Alzheimer's to find this useful with Faulkner.) Mostly he liked saying to the people who knew of our plans, "Well, these days, I'm reading *As I Lay Dying*," and watching their tongue-tied reaction.

A couple of mornings in a row, back in December, we had breakfast and discussed his memorial service. He said that the library was an okay setting and I knew that meant it wasn't perfect and I didn't try to do better. He said, Why don't I record a few remarks, or even a few poems. I could read the Szymborska poem and then you could play it over the loud-speaker. That'd get 'em, wouldn't it? I told him that that was a sadistic impulse and he shrugged amiably. So be it.

Except for stinginess or cowardice, there were no faults you could accuse him of that would hurt his feelings. On the other memorial-service details, we were in total agree-ment. Music: Bill Evans, of course. Poem: "Allegro Ma Non Troppo" by Wisława Szymborska. The sight of Brian, black fedora pulled down, crying in a small bookstore over a thick book of her collected poems, was one of the things that threw us into the massive disruption of our lives and our romance and our marriage and it does seem that there's not a sentence I can write that doesn't end with: and now he's dead.

Saturday, February 8, 2020, Stony Creek

I have spent some time thinking about what to wear for this memorial service. What I wind up with is very Sophia Loren at eighty: thin black coat over black jumpsuit, with a gold-buckled belt, black heels, a chic chignon, and you-lookin'-at-me sunglasses at 9 A.M., which is not a bad way to go but not what I thought I'd be doing.

Early in the morning, I drive over to my friend's house, who is also my hairdresser, and he puts my hair up. I could sit there, being loved and straightened and back-combed and sprayed, for hours. There is no place I'd rather be. Some of my dearest friends are coming, and some are not. I find that I have absolutely no bad feelings about those who don't. They have loved me and supported me and done the same for Brian, or not, and it doesn't matter anymore.

The memorial service is across the street from our house,

at the library. I love the library. The librarians are the way librarians should be: devoted to the books, kind but firm with the public. It has been awkward to arrange the service, since I knew we wanted it and I knew when we wanted it but I could not imagine saying to Alice, our librarian: Brian plans to die on January 30; could we book the library for February 8, between art shows and the yoga class? I don't remember how it comes to pass that the library is indeed booked for the service, but it is. My assistant and our friend, Jennifer, has probably arranged it, as she arranged the memorial cards. We are not having a Mass and we are not Catholic and we don't have a parish, but nevertheless, the memorial cards are a big hit. The card has a picture on one side of Brian, looking summer-sharp in his sunglasses, and a soaring hawk and few lines of Rumi on the other (*What is the body? Endurance. What is love? Gratitude. What is hidden in our chests? Laughter. What else? Compassion*). Everyone takes a card or two and I am a convert to them.

My friend Betsey will cater, because I cannot imagine a memorial service without food. (I am that kind of Jew—I cannot imagine a gathering of people that doesn't include food, and when I arrive at the WASP-y events at which you get a few sips of Riesling and a Ritz cracker, I am always disappointed, of course, but then a little bit impressed.) I'd rather feed people at the library than have everyone come back to the house. I know that some people will come back to the house come hell or high water, but if there is nice food at the library, people who didn't really know Brian may decide to pass on crossing the street and visiting with us and make the most of the library spread.

I walk over to the library before the service, and it is all muted chaos: Jack cannot figure out the sound system so we

can play Bill Evans. There's a problem with the microphone
that the minister needs to use. Betsey tells me that there are
not enough glasses. I don't remember how any of these things
are sorted out. I go back to the house and put on more lipstick
and I return to the memorial service, granddaughter Isadora
in tow. (Eventually the twins will come sit on my lap, as well,
and the three of them squirming for space and sobbing over
their beloved Babu is a great distraction. If I cried during the
service, I'd be surprised to hear about it.)

My daughter Caitlin is at the door to the library, guiding people into the community room. She looks enough like
me that for lots of people—our dentist, our former neighbors,
a college boyfriend—no other signage is needed. People will
come up to her for the next hour, to cup her face in their
hands, to look at her version of my face and turn left, as if
she's an actual sign, to ask for help in finding a seat, shedding
a coat. In twenty minutes, Caitlin will have to move out of the
lobby because there's no room, and people will gather, on this
sunny Saturday in February, outside on the library lawn and
in the corridors within the building, between the kitchen and
the restrooms. I never even see the people in the hallways or
those standing outside.

The first person I see in the chairs is my editor, Kate, sitting in her elegant, composed way, holding her coat, a manu-
script and a pencil on her lap, and editing while she waits,
which I find lovely and reassuring. I remember going to the
funeral of her husband, Forde, and the whole difficult year
after that, and I did wonder how she had managed then, and
seeing her in the folding chair, respectfully leaving room for
the reserved seats in the front rows, I'm ashamed to remember

that at the time I doubt I asked her more than twice about how she was doing. I know I did and said the stupid things that people do and say and I am resolved not to mind what anyone says today, no matter what.

(And there are some doozies, which I find cheering, even in the moment of receiving them. Many people remind me that he was too young, that it was unexpected, that they never knew he had Alzheimer's, that he surely had some good years left, and that I must be devastated. One person tells me that some days I will feel pretty good and other days, I'll want to die. Really die, she says.)

I recall my parents' memorial services, but they were very old people, had outlived most of their friends, and were in assisted living. We had no trouble accommodating everyone in their apartment. I knew that this would not be like that, but I am not prepared for the throngs of people showing up for Brian. My sister and her husband arrive early, and my sister looks vulnerable and ferocious, in her worry for me. People I expect to see and people I never expected to see fill the seats: his book club; his stained-glass teacher; a group of volunteers from Planned Parenthood, where he spent every Saturday morning escorting women from their cars to the clinic, always kind, always restrained, even when he itched to throw a punch at the screaming protestors. (It's such a great combination of my interests, he said.)

The next group of people to walk in are ten big white men, in navy-blue blazers and Yale ties, bulldogs or crests or Ys. Make way for the small fry, says one man, around Brian's size, pushing through the other, bigger men. He holds both of my hands and tells me that they all loved Brian. One man tells me he flew in from Arizona, and afterward he heads right back to the airport. Each man pats me or holds my hand and then they line up at the back of the room, shoulder to shoulder, legs apart, his sentinel. There is no transgression among them that I couldn't forgive.

Some of Brian's family come a little late and there is awkwardness over the seating, but everyone manages to be seated and our minister pulls us all together. I don't *have* a minister, but this minister is our friend, who married Brian and me in 2007. She had been Brian's minister during his Unitarian phase, and she was enough of a friend to me years ago to mention to me, when she heard he and I were serious about each other, that she thought Brian had a drinking problem and some wild ways. I didn't mind her telling me and she didn't mind marrying us a year later, so the friendship continued, and she gave a warm, affectionate, compassionate eulogy while gracefully introducing the speakers, and I kept thinking, as she spoke, Oh, darling, you would love this.

Allegro Ma Non Troppo

Life, you're beautiful (I say)
you just couldn't get more fecund,
more befrogged or nightingaley,
more anthillful or sproutsprouting.

I'm trying to court life's favor,
to get into its good graces,
to anticipate its whims.
I'm always the first to bow,

always there where it can see me
with my humble, reverent face,
soaring on the wings of rapture,
falling under waves of wonder.

Oh how grassy is this hopper,
how this berry ripely rasps.
I would never have conceived it
if I weren't conceived myself!

Life (I say) I've no idea
what I could compare you to.
No one else can make a pine cone
and then make the pine cone's clone.

I praise your inventiveness,
bounty, sweep, exactitude,
sense of order—gifts that border
on witchcraft and wizardry.

I just don't want to upset you,
tease or anger, vex or rile.
For millennia, I've been trying
to appease you with my smile.

I tug at life by its leaf hem:
will it stop for me, just once,
momentarily forgetting
to what end it runs and runs?

. . .

Three of his dearest friends speak about him. John Paul, his friend since the Seventies, evokes Brian the most for me. Their friendship transcended all kinds of differences, and their love of each other and of fishing bound them. John Paul speaks at length about Brian and their happy arguments and political discussions and at length about fishing, and even as part of me thinks, That's a lot too much about fishing, really—the other part of me feels that my husband and his long, boring stories about fishing have been beautifully brought to life, and I am so grateful. His friend Mark talks about their wanderings around New Haven and their big meals. He says that he asked Brian if he had any regrets in life and Brian finally came up with one regret: that he'd given away his vinyl-record collection. Mark says he was astonished that Brian had only one regret and it was that. I think, That's Alzheimer's for you, and then I think, Maybe not—my husband did not regret much, and wasn't that great?

His friend Tim talks about Brian's best big-brotherly qualities, Brian even going to watch Tim coach his high school lacrosse players, and there is love visible in the room. My mother-in-law, who had not planned to speak, comes to the podium and introduces herself and says that she has learned a lot about Brian today, his adult life in Connecticut, and I think she recognizes this in a way that is both lovely and sad.

His family will hold a second memorial service for him, in the Philadelphia suburb most of them call home. My sister-in-law calls to tell me that the service will be held in a Unitarian Universalist church. I'm pretty sure that none of the Ameches have ever been in a UU church for a religious service, except for Brian, and he stopped going twenty years ago. I take this decision to be a tribute to Brian, to his erstwhile affection for Unitarians. I suspect it is not a tribute to his fierce aversion to Catholicism and, in either case, I don't care. I am not as enthusiastic as my sister-in-law expects, I think, and it's a quick, awkward conversation. Later there is another one, from the other sister-in-law, who explains to me that although their beloved Father Bob wanted nothing more than to accommodate the well-connected Ameches (in the Seventies, the Ameches met with the pope, and the girls wore lace mantillas longer than their skirts and the group photo is amazing), the Catholic Church higher-ups would not allow a memorial service for Brian in a church. I think that perhaps it was because he chose his death, but I am assured that the Church, if not all for suicide, no longer holds it against the dead person or their family and it's not necessarily an impediment to Church burial. I wonder if it's me, and my mother-in-law laughs a little and says, with some embarrassment, that although Father Bob himself had no objection, his boss did worry that other people—more extreme members of the Catholic Church—might read of Brian's active support of Planned Parenthood and that *those* extreme people might behave badly. So, Unitarian Universalist church it will be, not as Brian would have wished (Yale Bowl, Sterling Library, the Trolley Trail near our house), but certainly nothing he would have objected to.

At the Pennsylvania service, almost all of the remarks are

about Brian as a child and a teenager. Lots of love, as he said once on a trip home to Philly, but I've been long gone.

Brian's life as an adult was not known to that crowd, but my mother-in-law's friends hug and kiss me and tell me what a handsome and lovely young man he was, and I bask. A lot of men in their sixties come up to me in the country club afterward, a steady stream of them following the service, to tell me about Brian's kindness and skill and smarts, even at eighteen. It pleased me and would have pleased him. "No one would knock you down harder or put out his hand to help you up faster," one man said, and I hugged him. I've picked an urn for Brian's ashes (skipping the ones with the Yale Y, the heron catching a fish, the hawk) and have a second one prepared for Yvonne. In one of our weekly conversations, she tells me that she didn't expect to love it, but she does. (Brian and I were not a morbid couple, but I have the ashes of both parents and my beloved Grandpa Bloom—I found his ashes in a Chock Full o' Nuts can in my father's old filing cabinet—in urns in our living room. I am happy to have them with me, and occasionally, when there's a big family celebration, one of the kids will move my mother's urn into the dining room, where the party is.) In December, I will put the beautiful cobalt-blue urn for Brian in a box in my closet for a very long time, hidden away, until I find the linden tree I want and can plant it on the little hill near our house and dig a hole for the urn at the tree's base. All spring, I'll study pictures of linden trees (popular in myths as a symbol of grace and protection) and then I'll put one in the yard and put a bronze plaque for Brian on the boulder near it.

· · ·

After the service in Stony Creek, when all the guests and
Ameches leave our house, it's dark. Everyone gets out of their
funeral clothes. It is me, my children, and their families, and
my friends Bob and Jack. I don't miss anyone or wish anyone
was there who is not, except Brian.

Saturday, September 15, 2007, Durham, Connecticut

Our wedding day. My mother isn't there to see it, and that is my only grief. The last time she was in the hospital, Brian dropped me off and went to park. My mother waved me into her room and kissed me. Is Brian coming up? she said. When I said yes, she practically pushed me off the bed and began firmly and pleasantly directing me in how best to help her: bed jacket, comb, blush, and lipstick, please. Hairspray. Hurry, please. By the time Brian came to her door, she was in full Greer Garson and sent me to get tea for both of them. Oh, she would have said over breakfast on our wedding day, isn't this lovely? Aren't you gorgeous? Isn't he the handsomest thing? She would have appreciated that, just as with my first wedding, my hair has been done up in a ghastly mid-century Priscilla Presley updo, and after the stifled gasps of my children and of my groom-to-be, who says, Wow, I've never seen

you look . . . that way, there's nothing to do but thank the updo
lady, brush it out (hard), and stick a few bobby pins in it, just
like last time.

Everyone who should be here is here. My father is frail and
kindly, and both things are still a surprise to all of us. My sister
and her family arrive early and support my father on all sides.
My older daughter and her fiancé, later to be her husband,
my dear Corey, who will arrive from Los Angeles just minutes
before the ceremony (and Eden and Ivy not yet thought of).
My son, Alex, and his wife, married just the week before (and
Isadora not even imagined). My younger daughter and a girlfriend (not the girlfriend who will become my beloved daughter-
in-law Jasmine, and Zora not yet even a light in anyone's eye).
I am in the midst of my brief TV life, and my agent and the
star of that show and my producer are all there. My producer,
who will be there for me, still, at every inch of Brian's life and
death, has ordered us an extraordinary wedding cake: trans-
lucent turquoise and silver sugar bubbles, cascading down the
silver and blue cake, pooling around the bottom layer onto a
large glass plate, like the Milky Way. Brian has approved every
aspect of the menu, huddling happily with the chef for a couple
of hours, and the day before, the two big men come to me grinning and say, We added a carving station, and of course they
did. I have gathered up every large scarf, shawl, and pashmina I
have, because it is a little chillier than I had hoped, and I've put
baskets of wraps on the front and the back lawn. It would please
my mother—because putting out baskets of wraps to keep your
guests warm is clearly making an effort.

Friends from all pieces of our lives are there: some neighbors who'd disapproved of our scandalous beginnings and

come around (we had both been with other people. We didn't
behave well. We fell in love and left our partners. We didn't
slink out of town, and we glowed like radium); all my shrink-
ish friends; lots of Ameches (who were hesitant about standing
under a chuppah with a Unitarian minister, but game); friends
from Brian's high school and college days; my friend Kay (the
one who'll accompany me from Zurich to Newark) and her
daughter, whom I've known since before she was born; one of
our favorite couples, who will divorce long before Brian dies,
and the half of the couple we keep will write him the most
beautiful platonic love letter ever; my daughters' pediatrician;
Brian's friends from fishing, and conservation, and local politics; our mother-daughter travel agents, who have become
friends but whom I never tell why we stop traveling; my dearest
people from Random House, who will become Brian's biggest
fans (at one in-house dinner, as people are showing enthusiastic support for a new book, I say: I know that when you
contemplate sending me out on tour, you all wish you could
send Brian instead—and no one disagrees); my most brilliant
friends and my kindest; the friends who were delighted by
Brian and me and the ones who were dubious, and worse;
friends whom I loved then and love now, some of whom I will
rarely see again, after this day, because time passes.

Our minister speaks wisely and warmly and I am delighted,
but I barely listen.

Brian takes my hands and I cannot see anything except his
face. He says, I prepared some . . . and then he squeezes my
hands tightly and he begins to cry.

"I love you so much," he says. "That's all I can say. I love
you so, so much and I will love you every day of my life."

Then he says, quietly, Your turn.

I say, Middle-aged women are supposed to look for the safe harbor, for the port in the storm of life. We are supposed to look for the calm and the comfortable. You are the port in the storm. And you are the storm. And you are the sea. You are the rocks and the beach and the waves. You are the sunrise and the sunset and all of the light in between.

I think I have more to say but I can't. We are holding hands, pressed against each other, holding each other up.

I whisper to him, Every day of my life, and he whispers to me, Every day of my life.

Acknowledgments

The beginning is Brian Ameche, who loved his life and me, his lucky wife, and was fearless, as always, in the face of the difficult decisions and cruel obstacles that preceded his death.

In my professional life, I am blessed to have Kate Medina, the true gold standard for editors and my own guardian angel, who helped me in every way with the most challenging book of my life. I am equally blessed to have the elegant, encouraging, thoughtful, and tenacious Claudia Ballard as my agent.

For research and assistance, practical, professional, and personal, I am very lucky to have the intelligence, insight, and support of Jon Logan-Rung and Olivia Weinshank.

Drs. Daniel Casper, Mary Jane Minkin, and Debra Nudel provided kindness and support.

Overwhelmed as I so often was, Dr. T. Wayne Downey, my psychotherapist, was not only a rock in a roiling sea, he was able to help me steer and find a version of solid ground. Likewise, the insightful and astute Susie Chang read my cards, offered sensible and sometimes inspired interpretation and observations.

My three readers for this work, three exceptional writers, Bob Bledsoe, Kate Walbert, and the late Richard McCann, made useful and important suggestions, with the deft touches and brilliance that mark their work.

My children and their families made it possible for me, and Brian, to get through this terrible time and to find comfort and beauty in our life and peace in his death. My beloved sister, Ellen, was even better and more supportive than she appears in these pages.

As ever, my assistant and friend, Jennifer, is to assistants as the sun is to the stars.

About the Author

AMY BLOOM is the author of *Come to Me*, a National Book Award finalist; *Love Invents Us*; *A Blind Man Can See How Much I Love You*, nominated for the National Book Critics Circle Award; *Normal*; *Away*, a *New York Times* bestseller; *Where the God of Love Hangs Out*; *Lucky Us*, a *New York Times* bestseller; and *White Houses*. Her stories have appeared in *The Best American Short Stories*, *The O. Henry Prize Short Stories*, *The Scribner Anthology of Contemporary Short Fiction*, and many other anthologies in the United States and abroad. She has written for *The New Yorker*, *The New York Times Magazine*, *The Atlantic*, *Vogue*, *O: The Oprah Magazine*, *Slate*, *Tin House*, and *Salon*, among other publications, and has won a National Magazine Award. She is the Shapiro-Silverberg Professor of Creative Writing at Wesleyan University.

amybloom.com
Facebook.com/AmyBloomBooks
Twitter: @AmyBloomBooks

About the Type

This book was set in Baskerville, a typeface designed by John Baskerville (1706–75), an amateur printer and typefounder, and cut for him by John Handy in 1750. The type became popular again when the Lanston Monotype Corporation of London revived the classic roman face in 1923. The Mergenthaler Linotype Company in England and the United States cut a version of Baskerville in 1931, making it one of the most widely used typefaces today.